SOUL MATES
by GOD

LET GOD BE YOUR MATCHMAKER

Brad and Nicole Tabian

myPraize, Inc.

SOUL MATES *by* GOD
LET GOD BE YOUR MATCHMAKER

Published by myPraize, Inc.
1900 32nd Ave. NE
Black Eagle, MT 59414

Details in some anecdotes and stories have been changed or combined for ease of reading and/or to protect the identities of the persons involved.

The names Brad and Nicole Tabian are pseudonyms.

ISBN-13: 978-1541343634
ISBN-10: 1541343638
Copyright © 2017 by myPraize, Inc.

SoulMatesByGod.com
SoulMates@myPraize.com

CONTENTS

APPENDICES

INTRODUCTION

Are you looking for that special someone to spend the rest of your life with? Maybe you've never been married. Perhaps your marriage ended in death or divorce. Whatever your circumstances, if you desire to find that unique person with whom you can share life, love and memories, then *Soul Mates by God* can help.

This book contains principles and insights that God taught me (Brad) during a decade of looking for and hoping that I would find the right woman whom I could love and cherish "till death do us part." My first marriage ended in divorce, and the heartbreak and problems that followed left me without any desire to remarry. But then there came the day when God encouraged me to consider marriage as a possibility again.

God's plan took me through various phases in order to get me ready to meet my soul mate. It wasn't easy or comfortable at times, but through this journey he was preparing me for his best.

As I re-entered the dating scene, I didn't have any idea of what to expect. Actually, I thought my options were pretty limited. I was no longer a young adult, and I figured I would be doing well if I could just find a Christian woman who wanted to marry me. This was the "beggars can't be choosers" phase.

During this time, I dated quite a few women. My relationship with a woman always started off great but ended when she came to the conclusion I wasn't right for her. It may sound crazy, but I wanted to marry each one of those ladies more than anything. However, something always brought the relationship to an end. Why was this happening? I was a committed Jesus follower who didn't want to be alone anymore. You would think God would have been more cooperative.

Over time I realized it wasn't up to God to cooperate with me. I had it turned around. I needed to learn how to co-operate with him when it came to this area of my life. But how?

I entered into the "teach me your ways" phase. I watched, listened and prayed. I continued to date, but something had changed in my approach to relationships. As I focused on God and his Word, I began applying to my relationships the princi-ples he was showing me. Instead of being a marriage zealot, I began to look at relationships from God's viewpoint and listen to what he was saying. I had been awakened to the fact that there was more to a good match than just finding another believer and experiencing chemistry.

Through my dating experiences during this time, God was showing me how different my situation really was. I need-ed more than "just" a Christian woman. It wouldn't be easy for someone to fit in with my life's work. I had a calling to a unique full-time ministry with many strategic responsibilities. My future mate would need to partner with me in what God had established during previous decades of my life or I would not be able to fulfill my current commitments. I needed a woman as unique as me.

As God made me more aware of the various choices in-volved in making a good match for me, I entered the "this will never happen" phase of dating. By that time, I had met a few ladies who were convinced *I* was God's man for *them*. But accord-ing to what God had been showing me, I knew it would be a mis-take to move beyond a friendship with any of them. I started to feel that if I were faithful to what God was teaching me and only married someone who fulfilled the criteria he had revealed to me, I would never marry. A match was impossible. On the other hand, if I compromised what God had revealed to me and got married anyway, I would live to regret it. I felt stuck and hopeless.

But then it happened! In the most unusual and unexpected way, I met Nicole. Nicole is a woman whom God custom-designed to fit me and my circumstances. A woman who completely satisfies the criteria God had shown me were necessary for me to have a God-honoring relationship. God made what was impossible, possible!

> "What is impossible with man is possible with God."
>
> —Luke 18:27

Nicole and I have now been married for five years. Every day we wake up and pinch ourselves because we are still enjoying married life so much. We continue to be amazed at new discoveries about each other. Every day our hearts are filled with gratitude that we both allowed God to be our Matchmaker.

We are living proof of God's promise that "every good and perfect gift is from above, coming down from the Father of the heavenly lights, who does not change like shifting shadows" (James 1:17).

In the pages that follow, Nicole and I will share what God has taught us about finding a soul mate and how to cooperate with the greatest Matchmaker of all time. We hope you will take these principles and insights to heart as you move forward in your quest for a mate. God knows you. He cares deeply about you and your desires. He has your future planned, and it is better than anything you can imagine! All you need to do is trust and follow him.

> "I know the plans I have for you," says the LORD. "They are plans for good and not for disaster, to give you a future and a hope."
>
> —Jeremiah 29:11, NLT

PART 1

BEGIN
YOUR
ADVENTURE

1

DISCOVER GOD'S BEST FOR YOU

Trusting the ultimate Matchmaker for
your special soul mate

I (Brad) remember the first time I met Nicole like it was yesterday. We had connected through an online dating service and had been talking on the phone most evenings for two weeks. This was in the days before FaceTime, so our interactions had been voice-only. We had decided to meet for lunch, and with some pre-date jitters, Nicole had suggested we not talk the night before the date so there would be something left to talk about when we actually met. I was already regretting that decision when, to my surprise, Nicole started what became an hour-long deluge of online messages zipping back and forth between us. After a hilariously fun time, and thirty messages later, we gave in and decided to talk anyway. The suspense of meeting in person the next day was electric.

We had decided on a lunch destination of Applebee's. Maybe it was coincidence, but we drove into the parking lot at the same time. Having never seen each other's vehicles, it was a surprise when I discovered that Nicole had pulled into the open space next to mine. I had seen her photos online, so as she got out of her car, I was pretty sure it was her. I got out of my car, and there she was! And then another surprise—she greeted me with a huge smile, followed by a hug. Wow!

That lunch was a wonderful continuation of what had been developing during the last few weeks. I was excited. Had I met my soul mate? Could it be that this encounter at Applebee's would be a life-changing event?

That was five years ago. Nicole and I will share more of our story in upcoming chapters, but for now, what about you?

Since you've picked up this book, we think we know something about you. You are probably single. Maybe you are widowed or divorced. Maybe you have never been married. Maybe you are young or only young at heart. But whatever your specific situation is, you are single ... and you'd like to be married. Maybe you'd r-e-a-l-l-y like to be married.

Have you ever considered the possibility that God already has a perfect match planned for you? If that's true, how can you cooperate with him to meet your future soul mate?

First, you must be willing to do things God's way and to patiently wait for his timing. God loves you and is committed to your well-being. He wants to guide your steps and choices so you can enjoy all the best he has to offer. God knows whether being married is a part of his ideal plan and purpose for you. And if it is, he also knows who will be your best mate. In fact, God is in the process of custom-designing and life-crafting that person just for you. Sounds incredible, right?

GOD'S WAY

Let's assume you believe God has a soul mate picked out for you. Great! You might be thinking, *I'm ready for a name and address.* But wait. This isn't just about you and your mate. God wants to be the focal point of your relationship. And because of that fact, he's not just going to drop a mail-order soul mate on your doorstep. Instead, he wants to take you on a personal journey that will transform you and result in a deeper love relationship with him.

When I was in my "beggars can't be choosers" phase (mentioned in the introduction), I was cheapening God's plan for me by placing insignificant value on the person who could most impact my future life. To me, just a few check marks on an extremely short list made most single Christian women candidates for this most important role. But God had greater plans than my shortsightedness. He wanted me to see my wife as a wonderful gift—as a tangible expression of his great love for me. I needed to expand my understanding of how God views me and how greatly he values my life. That's why he has given us the Bible—so we can clearly understand his desires, obtain an accurate perspective for reality and access the resources he offers us for this supernatural journey.

The Bible is God's road map to his best for your life. His commands are the guardrails. His principles are the signposts. His promises are the billboards describing the opportunities ahead. These are the spiritual truths and laws of the universe. And, like physical laws such as gravity, these spiritual laws can be ignored, but always to our peril.

In addition to giving us the Bible, God has also placed himself within believers in the person of the Holy Spirit. The Holy Spirit is our resident guide and counselor. He empowers us to do God's will and can transform us into the kind of person God desires us to be.

> Do not conform to the pattern of this world, but
> be transformed by the renewing of your mind.
> Then you will be able to test and approve what
> God's will is—his good, pleasing and perfect will.
> —Romans 12:2

God's supreme objective for you is that you continually love him more than any other person or any other thing. He wants to be the very center of your life—even after you have met the wonderful soul mate he has planned for you.

Wouldn't it be tragic if you became so preoccupied with God's wonderful gift of a mate that you ignored the Gift-giver? So, before you even meet your soul mate, God wants to use your life journey to get you ready for that relationship by reshaping your priorities and developing your character.

Do you realize our long-range well-being is a higher priority to God than our immediate happiness? As a result, he often withholds his planned blessings until we are mature enough to enjoy them appropriately. Unfortunately, we live in a culture that doesn't practice deferred gratification very well. In our impatience, many of us look for shortcuts to achieve happiness through our own methods and means. As a result, when it comes to relationships, we often find ourselves stuck in a bad predicament, experiencing the consequences of our foolishness and thoughtlessness.

Thank goodness God doesn't leave us to ourselves! Even when we make poor choices, when we confess our sins and call out to God for help, he will come to our rescue. Though we may have messed up his immediate plan for us through disobedience, God can still bring much good out of our bad situation (see Romans 8:28).

It stands to reason that if you choose to live your life using a natural decision-making process, you will get a natural result. However, if you use God's supernatural process, you will experience a supernatural result. But you can't do both at the same time. The choice is clear: either you trust God and do life his way or you rely on your own ingenuity and methods and live with those results.

GOD'S TIMING

Perhaps you are already trusting God for his best and following his directives, but you still have not met your perfect match. You may be wondering, *What's wrong? Why is nothing happening?* Well, something is happening; you just can't see it. God is quietly at work.

God's fulfillment of our desires is seldom immediate. It was God who first acknowledged that it wasn't good for Adam to be alone. But he waited to create Eve. First, God had Adam go through the process of naming all the animals in the Garden of Eden. Why? We believe that God wanted Adam to fully realize his need and to understand that, apart from God intervening, his personal need would remain unmet. When the time was right, God brought Eve into Adam's life. And when he did, Adam appreciated Eve and God all the more.

It was many years after my (Brad's) divorce before God prompted me to think about marrying again. And then God used many different relationships to make me wonder if I was ever going to meet someone who could be God's best for me. Why did that whole process take so long? Because it wasn't just about me reaching a marriage destination. It was also about the transformation that would occur in me during the journey. God wanted to change some of my attitudes and behaviors so I would be a better marriage partner. He also wanted to reveal more of himself to me and establish himself as my "first love" (see Revelation 2:4). He needed time to prepare Nicole for me as well.

Yes, there were many years of loneliness and disappointment. There were many Christmases and birthdays when I prayed that God would gift me with a mate. It seemed like nothing was happening. God was not responding like I wanted or like I thought he should. That was the problem. I was expecting God to respond to my wishes and desires, and he was waiting for me to learn how to respond to his.

But now that I am married to Nicole, I can tell you with great certainty—it was worth the wait! She is so much more than I ever believed was possible in a wife. I could never have imagined her. The bottom line? Father knows best! Our heavenly Father's ways and his timing are always right.

We would like to encourage you to see this soul-mate journey as your adventure with the God who is your Helper and Guide. In part 2 of this book, we will discuss the foundational prerequisites that are vital if you want God to be your Matchmaker. Part 3 will help you unload baggage that is potentially jeopardizing a future relationship. And in part 4 we'll discuss some practical dating strategies.

We pray you will find these principles and insights revolutionary in your quest for love and companionship. Focus on God and what he wants to accomplish on this journey. If you do, you'll arrive at your destination, not only with a soul mate, but also with a greater relationship with your heavenly Father.

2

MARRIAGE OR CELIBACY?

Does God have a custom-designed mate for you?

Do you ever wonder if God intends for you to get married? Maybe he wants you to remain single. Is it possible to know for sure what God's will is for you?

When God created Adam, he placed him in the Garden of Eden—a sinless, perfect environment. God and Adam enjoyed unhindered fellowship and Adam experienced an ideal relationship with his heavenly Father. Nevertheless, God makes a remarkable statement in Genesis: "It is not good for the man to be alone. I will make a helper who is just right for him" (2:18, NLT).

Even in this most perfect situation, God still wanted Adam to have a human soul mate, someone who was "just right" for him. It was not an oversight by God that he had to correct after reviewing his creation. God had always intended for Adam to have Eve—just not right away.

God established marriage as his norm for mankind; remaining single is the exception. Statistically, most people get married sooner or later, and that will probably include you. But how do you know you're not the exception? How do you know you're not in the minority of folks slated for a lifetime of singleness in the plan of God? Is it even possible to know?

Our view on the matter is that, while it may not be possible to know *for sure* that God intends for you to marry, it is possible to have a pretty good indication. Our goal is to help you not just marry anybody but find God's best for you—your ideal mate.

THREE TESTS

Assuming there is no obvious reason requiring you to remain single, the following tests will help you gain clarity about God's plan for you.

The Desire Test

As we've already discussed, our God is a loving heavenly Father who delights in giving us good gifts. He loves to fulfill our desires.

The Scriptures promise,

> Delight yourself in the LORD and he will give you the desires of your heart.
> —Psalm 37:4

> He fulfills the desires of those who fear him.
> —Psalm 145:19

In the light of these promises, it seems reasonable that if we really want to be married, God will grant that desire. This isn't an absolute guarantee, only a general assurance.

Some single people have never especially wanted to be married. Or if they did long for marriage at one time, their desire for it has waned. There's a good chance that God is not leading them toward marriage, because they don't have that desire anymore.

But most single people *do* want to be married. And since you've chosen to read this book, that likely includes you. You probably pass the desire test and are included in the majority of single folks who want to be married and can expect to have that desire fulfilled.

But let us point something out. It's important to judge whether your desire for marriage is a godly desire or a worldly desire.

Look closer at the verses quoted above. God gives people their desires if they *delight themselves in him.* He fulfills the desires *of those who fear him.* These promises are conditional upon being in a right relationship with the Lord. It's just like prayer—we can expect both our requests in prayer to be answered and the desires of our hearts to be fulfilled so long as they are aligned with God's will.

So ask yourself some questions:

- *Am I delighting myself in the Lord?*
- *Am I yearning to know God better and to love him more?*
- *Do I have a healthy fear of God, demonstrated by my reverential respect for him?*
- *Do I want to please, obey and trust God more?*
- *Is my heart becoming more centered on God and his purposes?*

If your honest answers to these questions reveal that God really isn't the top priority in your life right now, don't despair. Even if your desire to marry is rooted in selfish concerns, your heart and mind can be purified. The Holy Spirit can transform your longings so you will be more concerned about what God wants than what you want. When that happens, your selfish desires will be replaced with sanctified desires—desires that please God, desires that he wishes to fulfill.

When you have a yearning for marriage that grows out of your ongoing relationship with God, you have passed one important test suggesting that God wants you to be married. But there are two more.

The Calling Test

Scripturally, the single state in life is an honorable one. Daniel, Paul and—above all—Jesus are three biblical examples of people who were unmarried and close to God. If you're single, you're in good company indeed!

But consider for a moment *why* these three men were single. We think basically it was because their particular lifetime callings from God precluded marriage. God used Daniel to occupy a place of leadership in Babylon during the Jewish exile.

21

As a pioneering missionary, Paul was always moving around the region and could hardly maintain a normal family life. And then Jesus' mission, of course, was not to start an earthly family but to found the worldwide family of God.

In some specific situations, marriage can get in the way of our service to God. Paul explained it this way:

> I would like you to be free from concern. An unmarried man is concerned about the Lord's affairs—how he can please the Lord. But a married man is concerned about the affairs of this world—how he can please his wife—and his interests are divided. An unmarried woman or virgin is concerned about the Lord's affairs: Her aim is to be devoted to the Lord in both body and spirit. But a married woman is concerned about the affairs of this world—how she can please her husband. I am saying this for your own good, not to restrict you, but that you may live in a right way in undivided devotion to the Lord.
>
> —1 Corinthians 7:32–35

Paul seems to be echoing the Lord Jesus, who referred to some people who "have renounced marriage because of the kingdom of heaven" (Matthew 19:12).

As I (Brad) considered my own relationship with God and my commitment to full-time ministry, I wondered if God intended for me to live the rest of my life as a single person. My days were filled with many different responsibilities and I realized that if I were going to get married it might require major changes in my schedule. I also saw the possibility that a wife without similar values and priorities could create enough pressure in my marriage to cause me to leave my ministry calling. I truly believed God had shown me the criteria for a wife who would fit me and my unusual situation, but it seemed impossible that such a person existed. I began to doubt that my dream of being married would ever become a reality.

Then I met Nicole.

Nicole has a wonderful heart toward God and his people. In addition, I continue to be astonished at how God has gifted her with abilities, insights and a personality that perfectly complement my life and ministry. Since we've been married, not only have I not needed to make dramatic ministry changes, but Nicole has become a very insightful helpmate. We minister together and both feel blessed to have each other. I was delighted to discover that even a demanding life of service to God does not necessarily rule out marriage. If Paul had found a wife like mine, maybe he could have had a helpmate on his missionary travels! But still, I believe I was right in seriously considering the possibility that faithfulness to my calling might mean forgoing remarriage.

Every single person should take Paul's words seriously and ask himself or herself if marriage will advance or hinder a calling from the Lord. That's the second test, and there's one more.

The Passion Test

In that same passage from the apostle Paul (one that every single person should become familiar with—1 Corinthians 7), he said these things:

> Since there is so much immorality, each man should have his own wife, and each woman her own husband. (v. 2)

> To the unmarried and the widows I say: It is good for them to stay unmarried, as I am. But if they cannot control themselves, they should marry, for it is better to marry than to burn with passion. (vv. 8, 9)

> If anyone thinks he is acting improperly toward the virgin he is engaged to, and if she is getting

along in years and he feels he ought to marry, he should do as he wants. He is not sinning. They should get married. (v. 36)

So much immorality. Burning with passion. Acting improperly. These behaviors sound pretty familiar to a lot of single people today. Even though these words were written long ago, the Bible is amazingly relevant, isn't it?

So, let's be frank about it: If you're having trouble maintaining chastity as a single person, that may not be the loftiest reason for wanting to marry, but it's a legitimate reason. God knows the challenge you are facing, and in this case his escape route from temptation (see 1 Corinthians 10:13) may well be marriage.

So, here's a summary of these three tests.

Do you have a desire to be married?

Will your lifetime calling be enhanced if you marry?

Are you so desirous for a sexual relationship that your moral health seems to demand marriage?

We can't definitively speak for God about any individual's situation, but if you answered yes to more than one of the above questions, we believe the chances are that God does intend for you to marry sooner or later. Consider it and pray for God to give you confirmation in your heart.

If you determine that it is God's plan for you to marry, read on!

DOES GOD HAVE AN IDEAL SOUL MATE IN MIND FOR YOU?

Many Christian singles are wondering, *Does God have one particular person in mind for me? Or can I choose among many possibilities who have his approval?*

At a church we formerly attended, the pastor once preached a sermon that got our attention. He said from the pulpit, "Does God have a specific 'right answer' in mind every time you have to come to a decision? Does he want you to go to this college or that college? Take this job or that job? Move here or there? I don't think so. Not necessarily. If it's a moral decision, of course he wants us to do what is right. But if it's not, maybe he says, 'Whatever you choose is fine with me.'"

The pastor didn't mention the choice of a spouse, but he might as well have.

At the time of that sermon, the pastor's perspective was intriguing and rather persuasive to us. However, as we've thought about it more, we've come to question his view. We still believe that this pastor is a godly man, as are others who believe as he does in this matter, but we're not sure their perspective here is right.

We realize that we are getting into some rugged theological territory here. We're perilously close to the free will/predestination debate—and we don't presume that we'll resolve that one to everybody's satisfaction! But stay with us for a few paragraphs.

Doesn't the universe reveal God as a Creator who is intimately and intricately involved in his Creation?

Consider the human eye. It is made up of two million working parts processing thirty-six thousand bits of information every hour. The retina contains 120 million rods for night vision and 8 million cones that are color sensitive and work best in daylight conditions. It can distinguish five hundred shades of gray. Under the right conditions, a human being can see the light of one candle from fourteen miles away. And that's just one small organ!

Then there's evidence from God's Word. His own words reveal him as a God who cares about the details of our lives. When he was dictating the construction of the tabernacle, for example, he went so far as to specify the exact size of the incense altar and the specific number of fasteners to be used to hold the curtains. Also, in the laws he gave Israel, he instructed homeowners to build safety railings on their roofs and told them what to do when cattle trespassed onto someone else's property.

With these examples in mind, does it seem reasonable that God would take a hands-off approach about whom we might marry? We don't think so.

The word traditionally translated "help meet" to describe Eve (Genesis 2:18, KJV) means "a helper as opposite him." In other words, Eve was suited for Adam. It wasn't as if *any* woman would have served to meet Adam's unique needs. God made this *particular* woman *specifically* for him (just as God had earlier made Adam to be specifically suited for Eve). And we think he's still in the business of designing two people for each other in marriage. The God who numbers the hairs of our head knows what we need better than we do and generously provides it (see Luke 12:6–7).

Scripture describes all Christ followers as "God's workmanship, created in Christ Jesus to do good works, which God prepared in advance for us to do" (Ephesians 2:10). That is, God in his foreknowledge planned our role in the kingdom's work. Therefore, it seems likely to us that he also prepared a mate (for most of us) to help us fulfill the plan he has for our lives.

Having this perspective toward finding a mate offers all kinds of benefits. From the beginning, it causes you to become more engaged with God. Instead of just looking around for someone who seems appealing to you, you are trying to hear from God about his choice. Believing that your future mate is divinely intended for you causes you to enter marriage with higher expectations. You're not just thinking about your spouse, *Well, you'll do.* Instead, you're thinking, *What a wonderful adventure to see what God has planned for us together!*

So, contrary to what our former pastor preached, we believe that God has one person in mind for those of us he has called to marriage. Throughout the book, we refer to this person as "God's best for you" or "your soul mate" or "the right person" or "your ideal mate." The two of us often marvel at how well suited we are for each other and how God has crafted us to help each other along the road he planned for us. We hope that you, too, will find your intended spouse. It's a beautiful thing when you do.

Now, having said all of that, here is a word of caution.

We've been throwing around the word *ideal*, but just to make sure you understand—we're not talking about an ideal human being. Your "ideal mate" is the one person God most wants you to marry. He or she is not perfect, and living with this person in marriage will not always be easy. Nor will this person necessarily match up entirely with the image of a perfect spouse that you have formed in your mind. However, marrying this person will feel right, and you will have a sense of satisfaction in being married to him or her that you could never have had if you'd gone into marriage with anyone else.

But all this raises another question: Can you choose the wrong spouse? And what does it mean if you marry a man or woman who is not the person God wanted for you? It seems we can't get away from the theological speculation quite yet.

IS IT POSSIBLE TO CHOOSE THE WRONG SPOUSE?

We believe in God's foreknowledge, but we also believe in human free will. And that means that people *can* choose to marry someone whom God knew they would marry but who is not the ideal mate he could have designed for them.

Many times people jump into marriage without getting assurance from God that they are doing the right thing. Frankly, they don't care what God thinks, because they are so certain this person is right for them. Later, they may suffer the consequences of their foolhardiness. Often these marriages turn out to be difficult, sometimes ending in divorce. The marriage relationships might be over, but it doesn't erase the pain that was caused by the original mistake. Unfortunately, this is all too common, and for some it happens over and over. So much hurt, so much pain.

The poor choices people make in marriage remind us of Samson. This long-locked Hercules of the Old Testament saw an attractive Philistine woman and then came back to his father and demanded, "Get her for me. She's the right one for me" (Judges 14:3). But *was* she the right one? It doesn't appear so, because she let herself become the tool of his enemies and tried to take away his God-given gifts. She was the right one in Samson's eyes, but not in God's eyes.

However, the evidence surely seems to suggest that it's possible to choose a spouse who was not God's intended best for you but whom God can use for your best (see Romans 8:28). Since God is in the process of developing your character and your love relationship with him, he can use your present circumstances to accomplish his work. Never limit God with the realization of where you are in life. What is dark and dismal now might be the dawn before the gift of a new life together with your spouse.

And while we are giving words of caution, let us give you another caution. A strong caution.

We don't want to leave you with the impression that, if you think you have married someone who now feels like less than your ideal mate, it is okay to get out of that marriage and resume your search for the "right" person. That is foolish and destructive thinking. If a couple is married and experiencing difficulties in their relationship, they should ask God for his help to transform them and their marriage into what he desires. The path may be bumpy and challenging, but God still wants them to work toward unity and love.

Marriage is intended for life. Divorce is never God's plan. Whoever you are married to now is God's mate for you because God knew whom you would choose—whether that is his best or your alternative. But once you are married, there is no going back. In fact, because God knew everything you would do before you were born, he saw whether you would choose his best or not. If you chose someone else, then God didn't even bother to develop his ideal mate for you. Why would he? He certainly wouldn't want that person to miss out on his best just because you decided to go your own way. (Yes, there is no doubt—this is complicated!)

We'll put it another way: if two people are married, they

are looking at God's best for themselves *right now*. And that means that if they are married and someone besides their spouse looks like a better mate, they should beware. He or she is not God's ideal *mate* for them but Satan's ideal *bait*! Whoever else might once have been out there for them, they now have each other and should work on making their relationship all God intended for their marriage to be.

Sometimes, over time in marriage, one of the spouses becomes unfaithful to God and his or her mate. Perhaps the marriage ends in divorce. The question now is, *Does God have someone else for me?* Only God can answer that question. We know that God rewards faithfulness. But at the same time, unfaithfulness is a character flaw God will work to change, not transport into another relationship. If God is convinced that adequate repentance and character transformation has occurred, he is a God of mercy and second chances. Under those circumstances, only he knows if he will be Matchmaker for a future relationship.

It is important to remember that "in all things God works for the good of those who love him" (Romans 8:28). His overall plan is not thwarted by anyone's mistakes. Rather, he accommodates his plan in spite of his people's sometimes poor choices and keeps on working to do good things in and through them. He brings about victory in surprising ways.

One day we were talking to a friend of ours from India about arranged marriages. Paresh said, "In the West, most of your marriages start out hot and end up cold. In India, a lot of our marriages start out cold but end up hot." Isn't that interesting? Even a marriage where there is *no* choice on the part of the couple can turn out well!

Come to think of it, we don't need to look beyond the Bible on this matter. Jacob chose the wife he wanted—Rachel. But Jacob's father, Isaac, had his wife chosen for him—Rebekah. Both marriages were successful. That's what it's like when God is working out all things for good, and that's why there is always cause for hope.

EXPECTING THE IMPOSSIBLE

We've been through a lot of theological speculation in this chapter, and it's been necessary. But let's get back to being practical. If God wants you to marry, he's got an ideal mate in mind for you. So, how can you cooperate with God to discover his best for you—your divinely intended spouse? Where, oh where, is this person?

We know very well that a lot of single people are deep in doubt that they'll ever find the right person. Does that include you? Maybe you've been looking for someone for a long time. Maybe you feel like you'd be doing just great to find someone who is a Christian, who is a decent person and who likes you. Maybe marrying someone *designed just for you* seems impossible.

But let us tell you something: God's business is the impossible. I (Nicole) had become all but hopeless back in my single days. I met so many guys, but none of them were right for me. Then I met Brad. It took some time for me to really understand what God had brought me in Brad, because he didn't exactly fit my preconceived ideas about the ideal spouse. But eventually I knew he was right for me. And our years of marriage since then have proved to me that I wasn't wrong about that. I sold God short. Don't you do the same. Keep on believing that he's going to bring the right person into your life at the right time.

This is doable. We don't want you to get into paralysis, wondering every minute, *Is this the right person for me? What if I'm wrong?* No, it's like every other decision you make as a Christian. You cultivate your relationship with God and work on your ability to hear God's whispers. By taking your time, obeying God's Word and trying to sense his individual leading through the Spirit, you learn what he wants you to know.

Oswald Chambers once said, "The greatest enemy of the life of faith in God is not sin, but good choices which are not quite good enough. The good is always the enemy of the best." Don't settle for the merely good but instead wait for God's best for you.

Let God lead you. Examine the circumstances he's

putting you into. Consider the compatibility you might have with people he's bringing into your life. Be willing to give up your definition of *best* and embrace God's definition. Wait on his timing and trust in him. It will be well worth it.

PART 2

FIRST THINGS FIRST

3

IT STARTS WITH ME

*Becoming the right person so you can
meet the right person*

We will assume, at this point, that you must be a Christian if you are still reading this book. And since you are a believer, you are looking not just for any suitable person of the opposite sex to marry but specifically for the person of God's choosing. Whereas unmarried non-Christians might be dreaming of finding their type of ideal mate, you are dreaming of finding the ideal mate *from God's perspective.* In other words, you want God's best for you when it comes to marriage.

How did we do? Sum it up pretty accurately?

If so, we understand where you're at. We were both there at one time ourselves. And we know that many others are in the same situation—good Christian men and women who want to find a mate who pleases God and brings them companionship and enjoyment. We think that's an honorable desire. And it is for people with this desire that we have written *Soul Mates by God.*

So, here's the question: Are you ready for *God's best?*

We're guessing that you're not so sure you are. You haven't found the ideal godly mate—God's best for you—yet, and you're wondering if you're doing something wrong. Or at least if there is more you can be doing right. And that's where we can help.

YOU FIRST

We've got a big idea to try out on you. We're not here to give you tips on making a good impression on a first date. We're not offering you a deal to join an online dating club for only $49.95 a month. We're not going to advise you to downsize your weight, upscale your wardrobe, or polish your pick-up lines. Nothing like that. (What a relief, huh?)

In fact, instead of focusing on anything outward, like how you look or what you do, we're going to focus on something inward—who you are. And here comes the big idea.

When you *are* the right person, you'll *meet* the right person.

In other words, what we're suggesting is that, instead of focusing on *finding* your soul mate, you focus on *being* God's best for the person God has in mind for you. Of course, there's nothing wrong with actively looking for God's intended mate for you. There's a time for that. But there's something more fundamental, something that needs to come first. It's making yourself ready for that mate before you do find him or her.

Now for a couple of important clarifications.

First, by saying that you should strive to be the right person, we are not judging you in any way. We're not saying that you are not married because you are not good enough or not godly enough. Possibly, in some cases, God withholds a mate from somebody until he or she *improves* in some way, but certainly that is not always, or even often, the reason why someone is single. So please don't think we're assuming that you're inadequate.

And yet … And yet …

We're confident that you have room to improve. Why? Because you're human! We *all* have room to improve. Single or married, old or young, we all can be more like Christ. And after all, one advantage of not being married is that single people are generally freer to focus on their devotion to the Lord (see 1 Corinthians 7:34). At this point in your life, your singleness provides a great time to be working on becoming more of the man or woman God wants you to be. We don't want you to waste your present opportunity to grow in Christ. It's valuable whether or not you get married.

And that brings us to the second clarification. By suggesting that if you are the right person you'll meet the right person, we're not offering some kind of iron-clad, no-single-person-left-behind, money-back guarantee that you will find a mate, ideal or otherwise. God remains sovereign. It is possible that a mate is not in his will for you. Or at least not in his will for you right now. You should not try to be the person God wants you to be just so that he will give you what you want. Becoming Christlike is its own endeavor.

And yet … And yet …

We can offer you real hope because, as we discussed in the previous chapter, marriage is the norm and celibacy is the exception. That is, marriage is in God's plan for most people, and that probably includes you, sooner or later. It is especially likely to be true if you focus now on becoming the right person, for then you will be ready to meet the right person and move along to a godly and satisfying married life. The principles taught in this book have helped many people prepare for a terrific marriage. If you take them to heart, you'll be ready for God's best too.

LIVING TOWARD GOD

But all of this still leaves a question unanswered: What does it mean to be the right person? That's the key, isn't it? If we're saying that being ready to meet the right person depends on being the right person, what does that really consist of? Here's our answer: *Being the right person means living out God's purpose for your life.*

This is where being a follower of Christ is radically different from being an unbeliever. The world says, "Be your own man (or woman). Live life your way. Decide what you want and go for it." Is that what God wants from us? In a word, no.

Whether we're married or single, our purpose should not be to satisfy our own wishes but to do God's will. We're to love God more and more each day, know him better and better each day and follow him closer and closer each day. Living out God's purpose for us is a lifelong goal that takes work day by day, month by month and year by year.

This is exactly how Jesus operated. He said, "I and the Father are one" (John 10:30). That's hardly "be your own man." He said, "I have come down from heaven not to do my will but to do the will of him who sent me" (John 6:38). That's not "live life your way." Jesus lived out God's purpose for his life. He made his will align perfectly with the Father's will.

Permit us to ask you a personal question. Have you been praying for God to give you a mate? If so, maybe you're discouraged because the answer so far seems to be no. Maybe the letdown has even soured you on prayer altogether.

What if we said you could be confident of having your prayers answered? You can! Here's how: "This is the confidence we have in approaching God: that if we ask anything according to his will, he hears us" (1 John 5:14). The key words in this verse are "according to his will." We don't get what we want in prayer by bending God to our will through praying really, really hard. We get what we want by bending our will to God's, so that we pray for what he wants.

This is the essence of living out God's purpose for our life. We cultivate our relationship with him. We follow his standards and teachings. We come to want what he wants. We seek for him to be honored in all things and we try to fulfill his specific purpose for our lives. And in doing all this, we're at the right place to receive God's best for us at just the right time.

Seems simple, doesn't it? But it's easy to get tired of waiting. Boy, don't we know it! I (Brad) have already shared my story in the introduction of this book. Now let's hear from Nicole.

NICOLE'S STORY

I was never married before I met Brad. Instead, I spent years and years in dating relationships, some long term, many short term.

At first, dating was just fun for me. I had my eyes open

for the man God had for me, but I wasn't in any particular hurry. I was sure my husband would come along. But then he didn't … and didn't and didn't. Even though I dated some great guys, the relationships never lasted. I began to get impatient. I became the kind of desperate, needy woman who turns men off. I wanted to be married, and I wanted to be married *now*!

One day I talked to an older woman in my church who was a mentor to me. She asked me, "Why are you in such a hurry to be married?"

"Well, because I'm lonely," I replied, "and I want to have kids."

"Do you think God knows what's best for you?"

"I suppose so."

"Well, don't you think that means he knows the best timing for your marriage? Take some advice from someone who's been around longer than you. I look back and I see lots of things I didn't get when I wanted them—and now I'm *glad* I didn't. I've realized that most of those things wouldn't have been good for me right then. Relax. Keep following God and trust him to bring the right man into your life at the right time."

To be honest, that advice annoyed me at the time. Even though it sounded reasonable, it wasn't what I wanted to hear. And besides, how do you make yourself "relax" and "trust"?

But that conversation did make me think about some of my friends who had rushed into marriage when they shouldn't have. Each situation was somewhat different, but all of my friends so wanted to get married that they were blinded to what their boyfriend or girlfriend was really like. They moved too fast. They didn't wait for God's best for them. And now they are either divorced or trying to make the best of a bad marriage. As much as I disliked being single, I didn't want to be like them!

My mentor was right. God sees the big picture. He's in no hurry. He always brings into my life what's best for me when he wants and how he wants. My wisest choice is just to cooperate with him.

I finally had a heart-to-heart talk with God. I got down

on my knees and prayed something like this: "God, I still want to be married, and I know you know I want to be married. I'm going to trust that, for right now, being single is what you want for me. I pray that you'll bring the right man to me at the right time."

Eventually I met someone in a most unusual way. His name was Brad. The rest is history!

THE BASIS OF HOPE

With a new perspective, everything changes though nothing is different. Isn't that true? In different ways, the two of us learned to give up our narrow perspectives and adopt God's perspective instead. As single people, we still wanted to be married, but we figured out that first we needed to get ourselves in line with what God wanted for our lives as a whole. Then the marriage he wanted for us—God's best—would fit in with that.

We think this is a message many single people need to hear. You want God's best in a mate? Great! Don't try to find a mate on your own. God will reveal him or her to you when you're ready.

God knows you completely. He knows the person he has in mind for you. He knows what's coming up in the future. He knows what's best for you spiritually. And he's not blinded by the urgency you may feel. He's not thinking about short-term happiness but about what's best for you in the long run. He'll give you just the right mate if you are following him.

Chances are, someone else is out there looking for you. Now is your chance to become God's best for him or her. Spend time seeking God so you can begin to know the purpose he has for your life.

Many single people focus all their energy on searching for their mate. But if God knows you are not yet ready to meet him or her, why would he help you find this person prematurely? It makes much more sense to concentrate on becoming the person God wants you to be, and then he will more quickly become your Matchmaker.

In the rest of the book, we'll be looking at ways you can cooperate with God so you are ready to receive his best in a mate. You'll find foundational concepts in the following chapters that will provide answers to these key questions:

- Am I truly a candidate to receive God's best? (chapter 4)
- Do I have the right ideas about marriage? (chapter 5)
- Why should I believe that God will give me his best? (chapter 6)
- Where can I get the help I need to become ready for my soul mate? (chapter 7)
- How can I cooperate with God on the journey toward happiness in the marriage he has for me? (chapter 8)

Each one of these chapters goes deeply into spiritual truth. They provide biblically based insights that you can use in many areas of your life, most certainly including your romantic life. We urge you to take the time to lay a good foundation. Our promise is that you won't regret it and you'll never be the same afterward.

4

ARE YOU QUALIFIED?

*Making sure you're on the right path
to receive God's best*

Did you ever do a pencil maze as a child? If so, you remember using your pencil to make a line from an entry point to (you hoped) the goal at the center of the maze. But if you moved your line down the wrong part of the maze, you wound up at a dead end and had to go back and start over again, maybe only to come up against another dead end. Frustrating, wasn't it?

We want to help you avoid the same kind of wasted effort in your pursuit of a godly marriage. We want to make sure you're on the right path to start with. You see, before you can meaningfully ask the question of whether you're ready to receive God's best in marriage, you have to decide if you are even a candidate for God's best in the first place. Not everyone is.

Now, certainly everyone receives good things from God's hands. As Jesus himself said of the Father, "He gives his sunlight to both the evil and the good, and he sends rain on the just and the unjust alike" (Matthew 5:45, NLT). Some theologians call this God's *common grace*. He gives many blessings of life to believers and unbelievers alike.

But God reserves his *best* blessings for his dearly loved sons and daughters (see Matthew 7:9–11). We're talking about the blessings of eternal life, the presence of the Holy Spirit, membership in the family of God and a chance to help advance

God's grand plan for history. What wonderful opportunities! "What great love the Father has lavished on us, that we should be called children of God!" (1 John 3:1).

Another one of the for-God's-kids-only blessings is what we have been calling "God's best" in marriage. Remember, this is not just any marriage. It is not even just a happy marriage. Rather, it is a marriage that represents God's highest will for our most intimate human relationship. This relationship doesn't just bring us enjoyment but also furthers God's purpose in our lives. Such a marriage is something that God works out only for his sons and daughters who know and follow him faithfully.

Does that include you? Let us suggest five questions you can answer to find out. The first one is the most important.

QUESTION #1: DO YOU KNOW GOD PERSONALLY THROUGH JESUS CHRIST?

Some people think that everyone is automatically accepted by God and is a candidate to receive his best. Others think that, while perhaps not everyone is accepted by God, nevertheless the standards are low and there are many paths to divine acceptance. Is this true? We're afraid not. But don't take our word for it; take Jesus' word. He said that the gate that leads to eternal life is a narrow one and few find it (see Matthew 7:13-14). This is the key: Jesus is the gate! We come to God through faith in Jesus Christ alone ... or not at all (see John 14:6).

It's important to answer this question correctly, so think about it seriously. Consider these words from Jesus and the Bible:

> "I am the way, the truth, and the life. No one can come to the Father except through me." (Jesus speaking)
>
> —John 14:6, NLT

> Salvation is found in no one else, for there is no other name under heaven given to mankind by

which we must be saved.

—Acts 4:12

To all who believed him and accepted him, he gave the right to become children of God. They are reborn—not with a physical birth resulting from human passion or plan, but a birth that comes from God.

—John 1:12–13, NLT

It is by grace you have been saved, through faith—and this is not from yourselves, it is the gift of God—not by works, so that no one can boast.

—Ephesians 2:8–9

Thinking you have a connection with Jesus and doing religious stuff, even really impressive religious stuff, doesn't guarantee that you have eternal life. You have eternal life only if you really *know* Jesus personally, as demonstrated by inviting him into your life, accepting the penalty he paid on the cross for your sins and giving him the right to make you the kind of person he wants you to be.

Now answer: do you or don't you know God for real? If so, that's wonderful. If not, why not change your answer right now? You can begin a relationship with God today through humbling yourself, turning to Jesus in faith and committing your whole life to him. Pray a prayer like this:

Lord Jesus, I need you. Thank you for dying on the cross for my sins. I open the door of my life and receive you as my Savior and Lord. Thank you for forgiving my sins and giving me eternal life. Take control of the throne of my life. Make me the kind of person you want me to be.

Personally knowing God through Christ is the essential first step to receiving God's best. It's the channel to the center

45

of the maze. But that's not all. It's been said that getting saved isn't the purpose of biblical faith any more than admissions is the purpose of a university. Getting saved is just the beginning. After that comes—or at least *should* come—a whole life of knowing and serving God. And that is what the next four questions address.

QUESTION #2: IS GOD NUMBER ONE IN YOUR LIFE?

Jesus said that you can know his true followers by their "fruit"—what they do with their lives (see Matthew 7:15–20). Godly people, though not perfect, do godly things. There ought to be *something* visible, *something* tangible about their lives to demonstrate their faith if they are truly following him.

If we want to receive God's best, we should not just minimally have a relationship with him through his Son but should be pursuing him with everything in us.

Let us introduce you to our friend Angela, who is a member of the singles group at our church. As leaders of this group, we're honored when members of the group ask our advice on issues in their lives. One day, Angela, who was twenty-eight years old at the time, asked to speak with Nicole privately. Angela was a woman we saw only occasionally at the group, usually when she was between boyfriends. On this occasion, Nicole could tell at once that Angela was discouraged.

NICOLE: What's up, Angela? You don't look like you're in too good a mood.

ANGELA: Steve broke up with me.

NICOLE: Oh. Sorry to hear that. I never met Steve.

ANGELA: I could only get him to go to church the one time.

NICOLE: I see.

ANGELA: Do you think God will ever give me a husband?

NICOLE: I can't say for sure, but actually I do think so, yes.

ANGELA: What am I doing wrong? Do you think I need clothes?

NICOLE: Maybe you're focusing on the wrong things, Angela. I mean, maybe you should be working on who you are on the inside, your spiritual life.

ANGELA: What do you mean? I'm a Christian. I have been ever since summer camp when I was twelve.

NICOLE: That's great to hear. But twelve was a long time ago. What's your relationship with God like now?

ANGELA: I come to church … when I can. I pray … sometimes.

NICOLE: Well, that's a start. But you know, Angela, I sense that God has so much more in mind for you. I think he wants to make you into a woman who's radiant with his love and presence. You're a natural leader. I think you could be used to draw others to God. And if you were in that kind of place in your relationship with the Father, then there's every reason to believe he would lead you to a young man who was just as much in love with him as you are. What do you think about that?

Angela had a look on her face like she was trying hard to figure out what Nicole was getting at.

If you've spent much time reading the Old Testament, you know that over and over the Israelites got off track in their relationship with God through worshiping other gods. God made it clear to them from the start that he was the only true God, and he warned them that worshiping idols would have dire consequences for them. But somehow it was just too tempting to turn to the false gods their neighbors were worshiping.

We can easily slip into the same error. If we put anything else besides God as number one in our lives, we are making an idol of it and we are putting ourselves in jeopardy. For single people, one of these potential idols is wanting a mate. Hopefully this isn't true for you. But we've known people who were so focused on finding a husband or wife that they were ready to ignore God and his teachings. Is this what God wants of us? For that matter, is this what our hoped-for godly mate would want to see in us?

Get your priorities straight. You must first seek the kingdom of God and his righteousness, and then he will give you his best (see Matthew 6:33).

QUESTION #3: ARE YOU LEARNING MORE ABOUT WHO GOD IS?

Your relationship with God can't be all God intends, and you can't be in a position to receive his best, unless you know who he is. And the best place to learn more about God is from his Word the book that God inspired to teach us about himself.

One great way to learn more about God is to study his attributes, which are the qualities that define what he is like. In his book *God: Discover His Character*, the late Bill Bright defined God's key attributes like this:

God is a personal Spirit.
God is all powerful.
God is present everywhere.
God knows everything.
God is sovereign.
God is holy.
God is absolute truth.
God is righteous.
God is just.
God is love.
God is merciful.

God is faithful.

God never changes.

Which of these attributes is intriguing to you? Which do you not know much about? Embark on a personal Bible study to get to know God better in these key areas (see Online Resources, page 201).

God has the ability to do anything he wants to do, the integrity to always do what he has promised and the commitment to pursue your personal well-being. God is able, trustworthy and loyal—he wants to guide you to your best future.

QUESTION #4: ARE YOU DEVELOPING A MORE INTIMATE RELATIONSHIP WITH GOD?

Head knowledge about God from the Bible is important. But so is heart knowledge—what you learn about God by living with a heart open to him day after day. Have you perhaps lost your first love for God (see Revelation 2:4)? Get it back by restoring or starting habits in your life that will rekindle that love.

Pursue God. Just as you pursue a person of the opposite sex you have an interest in, so you should pursue God. What are you willing to invest in your pursuit of God? Seek him, draw near to him, wait on him, and he will reveal himself to you.

Trust God. God is completely trustworthy. There is no one who cares more about you. There is no one who has greater abilities. There is no one who can guarantee promises made to you with more integrity. What are you willing to entrust to God today because you have faith in his character, capabilities and love for you?

Enjoy God. Our God is invisible, but his daily involvement in our lives and presence is obvious to a discerning observer. There are several ways you can enjoy God moment by moment throughout every day. How has God recently demonstrated his love and goodness to you? Did you notice God controlling circumstances? Did God intervene to get you out of a negative situation? Did God provide for a need? Did God protect you from harm or evil? Did you become aware of an answer to a specific prayer? Thank him and revel in his love.

QUESTION #5: ARE YOU SERVING GOD AND SEEING HIM BLESS YOUR SERVICE?

Putting God first, getting to know him better, developing an intimate relationship with him—these are all crucial to having a quality relationship with God. But there is at least one more major area to consider. It's what you do with your life as a result of your connection to God.

A part of this service is obedience to his commands. God has guidelines and commands for us and expects us to follow them. We move toward holiness by living according to his expressed will in moral matters.

But there's another, more adventurous part of serving God—finding and fulfilling your personal mission in life. God may have gifted you to evangelize others within the business community. He may have designed you to nurture young children. Angela has leadership potential that makes her influential to others. The possibilities are endless. But whatever your God-given purpose in life, fulfilling it is one way of becoming the man or woman he intended you to be and a candidate for receiving his best.

The apostle Paul sums it up like this:

> I plead with you to give your bodies to God because of all he has done for you. Let them be a living and holy sacrifice—the kind he will find acceptable. This is truly the way to worship him. Don't copy the behavior and customs of this world, but let God transform you into a new person by changing the way you think. Then you will learn to know God's will for you, which is good and pleasing and perfect.
>
> —Romans 12:1–2, NLT

A TURNING POINT

A couple of months after Angela and Nicole had their conversation, Angela agreed to accept some discipling from Nicole. She's working on making God her top priority and using her head, her heart and her hands to improve her relationship with him. We don't know what the outcome will be yet. But we believe she's at last on her way to a life filled with fruitfulness for God and a new richness of blessing in her relationships.

What about you? Are you on the right path to receiving God's best? You are if you know God through faith in his Son and are also actively cultivating your relationship with him through whatever means you can! Keep on cooperating with the Holy Spirit so he can bring about the necessary changes in you to get you ready for your ideal mate.

5

CHANGE YOUR PERSPECTIVE

Letting God's Word determine how you think

Dating, courtship and marriage can be confusing matters. Wouldn't it be great to know the decisions you are making in these areas are based on real truth? That the perspective you hold on to is grounded in reality?

But what, in today's world, can we rely upon as a source of truth? Friends? Family? The media? History? The Internet?

In order to discover truth for our lives, we must begin by committing ourselves to something we can rely upon for providing a foundation of truth. Only the Bible can be trusted to provide us with real truth. We need a *biblical view of life*, a perspective that is based on the Bible—on God's truth.

A biblical worldview is grounded in a commitment to knowing and understanding the Bible. It is a commitment to ascertaining truth for our lives and applying that truth to the everyday situations we encounter.

Unlike the Bible, however, "the wisdom of this world is foolishness in God's sight" (1 Corinthians 3:19). Unfortunately, many Christians live their lives based on the deceptive philosophies of this world. Although they are saved, their lives are filled with the consequences of ignorance and foolishness.

If something feels right but God's Word says it is wrong, we need to go with the Bible. For example, it might seem to make sense to have sex before marriage or to marry an unbeliever. But the Bible clearly states that these things are wrong, so Christ's followers should not even think about doing them.

If we want to experience God's best in life and marriage, we must first make sure that our core convictions are consistent with the truth he has revealed to us in the Bible. Believers must use the Bible as the ultimate authority for daily living and be committed to renewing our minds with biblical truth.

A SHARED OUTLOOK

Since in this book we're considering how to find God's best in a soul mate, let's consider something else when it comes to decision making: it's important that you be looking for a mate who shares your point of view regarding life—the biblical worldview.

The Bible says that, in marriage, two people become one (see Genesis 2:24). That oneness has many dimensions, not the least being spiritual oneness—an agreement in your core beliefs about God. You won't have found God's best unless you achieve spiritual oneness.

Spiritual oneness is cultivated by having the same foundational beliefs and philosophy of life. This doesn't mean that you agree with your future spouse on everything. But it does mean that you have the same starting place—the truth of God's Word.

I (Brad) am reminded of a friend whose first marriage was a disaster. Taylor said one of the most important things he learned from that experience was the importance of having a shared biblical worldview in a marriage.

You see, his wife Kara had a worldview (everyone does), but it wasn't a biblical one. It was a worldly one. Essentially, her attitude was that she should be living for whatever brought her the most happiness. It's not that she was a bad person, but she had put herself, not God, at the center of her universe. Meanwhile, Taylor—while far from being an ideal follower of Christ— was at least striving to serve God and follow his teachings.

Conflict was inevitable. For example, Taylor wanted

them to give a regular portion of their income to the church. Kara thought this was insane. She objected so much that Taylor gave in to her, and they held on to their money. He believes now that this was one reason God did not bless them financially in those days.

Kara and Taylor were not in agreement on how they were going to live life because they had different worldviews. Taylor had a more biblical worldview, while Kara had a more worldly worldview.

I thank God that Nicole and I share the same Bible-based outlook on the important things. We're still different people. In some ways, really different! But we do have a shared commitment to God's view of the truth in Scripture. When an issue comes up that we are not sure about—politics, environmentalism, gender roles or whatever—we go to the Bible to reconcile our differences.

This is a key compatibility issue. Take a tip from us: Plan to marry someone who uses the Word of God as their authority.

LIGHT OR DARKNESS

For a single person, having a biblical way of thinking is not just a nice option if you feel like it. It's crucial to making the choices that will bring happiness later. Having a biblical worldview is important for you now, as a single person searching for God's best in a mate. You won't know how to get ready for God's best unless he tells you how. The choice of one's viewpoint, and the other choices that flow from it, really make a difference.

The fact is, truth leads to blessing, while falsehood leads to pain. If you've been hurt in your dating life, we would just about be willing to bet that it was partly due to your believing a falsehood instead of following truth. You don't want to continue down that road, do you? Of course not … and you don't have to.

To explain what we're talking about, we want to go to what might seem a rather obscure Bible passage:

Your eye is the lamp of your body. When your

eyes are healthy, your whole body also is full of light. But when they are unhealthy, your body also is full of darkness. See to it, then, that the light within you is not darkness. Therefore, if your whole body is full of light, and no part of it dark, it will be just as full of light as when a lamp shines its light on you.

—Luke 11:34–36

What in the world does all this mean?

Just as light comes in through our eyes so that we can see things, so ideas come in through our mind so that we can understand the world. Thus, the quality of those ideas matters. Some people think they have the light of truth inside them, but that "light" is really darkness because their "truth" is really falsehood. They've got a worldly worldview. Only when our understanding is formed by God's truth can we be filled with true light.

Let's go back to the two examples we mentioned earlier: having premarital sex and marrying an unbeliever. Both can seem right from a worldly perspective, but that "light" is darkness. Premarital sex has been proved over and over to lead to such problems as a damaged relationship with God, difficulty committing in marriage and the risk of disease. Marrying an unbeliever sets up an endless series of conflicts and carries the strong probability that the unbelieving spouse will pull the believing spouse further from God instead of the believing spouse moving the unbeliever toward him.

Having a biblical worldview, and making decisions accordingly, really makes a difference. It's a question of ...

Light or dark.

Truth or falsehood.

Godliness or worldliness.

Happiness or suffering.

God's best or God's worst.

As we think about how a biblical worldview influenes our choices, we want to suggest two other ways in which a worldview has important practical effects for a single person who's hoping to be married. The first has to do with the way that many single people *look at themselves*. The second has to do with the way that many single people *look at God*.

YOUR IDENTITY AND VALUE

Sadly, we've known many single people, especially ones who have been searching for a soul mate for a long time, who feel badly about themselves. Maybe they hate the way they look. Maybe they think they are no fun, don't make enough money or don't have any personality. Since they haven't found God's best in the form of a mate yet, they have begun to assume that something is wrong with them. And they fear that they are thereby disqualified from ever having a soul mate. Is this kind of feeling legitimate?

Well, of course there are always ways that any of us can improve ourselves. In a sense, that's what this book is all about. But let us say this to you: if you are a Christian, your identity is absolutely secure and undeniably valuable.

Let's see what Scripture says about you.

First of all, you were made in the image of God. You're not living in this world by chance, the product of impersonal processes. You reflect the very nature of God.

> God created mankind in his own image, in the image of God he created them; male and female he created them.
> —Genesis 1:27

Second, your body was specially crafted by God and is beautiful. There is no one else like you. Think of all that your mind and body can do! You're a miracle made by God.

> You created my inmost being; you knit me together in my mother's womb. I praise you be-

57

cause I am fearfully and wonderfully made; your works are wonderful, I know that full well.

—Psalm 139:13–14

Third, God has a plan for you and is carrying it out. Just like Jeremiah (see Jeremiah 1:5), you have had a role prepared for you even before you were born.

All the days ordained for me were written in your book before one of them came to be.

—Psalm 139:16

We are God's handiwork, created in Christ Jesus to do good works, which God prepared in advance for us to do.

—Ephesians 2:10

Never believe the lie that you are a mistake or you are not good enough. You are made in God's image, redeemed by Christ's blood and held secure in his hand for all eternity. You are exactly the person God designed you to be. And more than that, you are a person God loves.

GOD'S LOVE AND GENEROSITY TOWARD YOU

Many single people we know think that they haven't found a soul mate yet because God doesn't care about them. They may even think he is punishing them for something they did wrong in the past.

Nothing could be further from the truth! Whatever the reasons may be for your not being married, it is not because God doesn't love you or because he doesn't want to give you good things. A biblical mindset believes the exact opposite.

Savor these scriptures on God's love and generosity for you:

"I know the plans I have for you," declares the
LORD, "plans to prosper you and not to harm
you, plans to give you hope and a future."

—Jeremiah 29:11

I have loved you with an everlasting love.

—Jeremiah 31:3

Neither death nor life, neither angels nor
demons, neither the present nor the future, nor
any powers, neither height nor depth, nor anything else in all creation, will be able to separate
us from the love of God that is in Christ Jesus our
Lord.

—Romans 8:38–39

See what great love the Father has lavished on us!

— 1 John 3:1

God *does* love you and wants you to have his best. He
has so many good things in store for you in this world and the
world to come. In all likelihood, one of the good things he wants
to give you in this world is a loving spouse. But to be ready to
receive that gift, you first have to believe that God wants to give
it. You have to believe what Scripture says, not what your worst
imaginings suggest.

IMMERSED IN THE WORD

So, how do you get a biblical worldview? By letting the Bible
speak to you more consistently and more influentially than the
world speaks to you. Let the words of God wash over you day
after day. You can't help but be changed if you are willing to do
that!

Consider these ways to let Scripture change you:
- *Read it devotionally.* Have a quiet time of Scripture
  reading with prayer every day.
- *Discuss it.* Join a small group or class where the

Scriptures are discussed. If you're dating, read and discuss the Bible with your boyfriend or girlfriend.

- *Study it.* Buy Bible reference books and learn from those who have studied in the past. Take a class at a Bible college or seminary.

- *Memorize it.* Select key passages and "hide them in your heart." Bring them up when you or someone else needs them.

- *Meditate on it.* Choose a short passage and ponder every phrase. What does it mean? How does it apply to you?

- *Pray it back to God.* Use lines from Scripture in your prayers.

- *Listen to it read.* Get an audio Bible and listen to it while you're driving or taking a walk.

- *Listen to it preached.* Go to church to hear Bible-based sermons and take notes. Listen to reliable Bible teachers on television, on the radio and over podcasts.

- *Sing it.* Whether at church or on your own, sing spiritual songs based on Scripture.

- *Teach it.* They say that teachers learn more by teaching than their students do, so pass on what you learn about the Bible.

- *Apply it.* Obey God's Word. This is to make it active and to reap the rewards of a biblical worldview.

We believe that if you have been living by a worldly mindset, you can make a change. You can deliberately saturate your mind with God's truth so that your decision making and your very thinking will be different. You'll be living a life of wisdom and not foolishness. And then you will be ready to recognize the mate God intends for you and go on to pursue him or her in a way that results in a satisfying, lifelong marriage.

6

DEVELOP THE RIGHT GODVIEW

Seeing God as he really is

"What comes into our minds when we think about God is the most important thing about us," wrote A. W. Tozer. Is that really true? We think it very well may be. If your view of God is distorted severely enough, it could ruin your spiritual health, your relationships, your decision making—even your whole life. On the other hand, if your view of God is correct and you are growing into more understanding of him, then you know who you are dealing with in the spiritual realm. And you can learn how to relate to him properly.

This is why we believe that, if you want to make yourself ready for God's best in marriage, you not only need a biblical worldview (as we discussed in the last chapter), but you also need what we call a biblical "Godview." You need to know who God really is. Without a true perspective on God, you can never have a true perspective on yourself and your love life desires.

To convince you that this is true, let us first introduce you to two unmarried acquaintances of ours whose Godviews went askew in radically different ways.

Joshua thinks God will let a person get away with just about anything. We speculate that this attitude goes back to the fact that he was a "trust fund baby." His grandfather wasn't particularly involved in his life, but being a very wealthy man, the grandfather set aside enough money for young Joshua so that he could pretty much live as he liked without working. Which is just what Joshua has done to this day.

Joshua is a Christian, or at least says he is, but for whatever reason, he's got the notion that God is distant and indulging. In Joshua's way of thinking, God—instead of issuing commandments—offers suggestions. Instead of condemning wrongdoing, God rolls his eyes as if participating in the joke about the mischief that's been made.

And mischief making is just what Joshua is known for. Now thirty, he's been playing with the hearts of young women for years. He talks his girlfriends into getting into bed with him or drops them if they refuse. He leads them on about getting married and never commits to them. We've known him to date two or even three women at a time without telling them about each other.

Is there any guilt weighing on Joshua's conscience about all this? It doesn't seem so. And why should it? In Joshua's view, God isn't the sort of deity who really cares about what Joshua does. Joshua's girlfriends are paying the price for his distorted Godview.

Maria, in sharp contrast to Joshua, thinks God is maliciously withholding marital happiness from her. The failed relationships, the two broken engagements—they're God's way of getting back at her for her sins. She doesn't blame God, mind you. She resents him, probably, but she thinks that making life difficult for her is what he's supposed to do. Like a judge, he's in the business of scrutinizing her every move and laying down swift punishment for every infraction.

We don't know what it is in Maria's background that led to this attitude. Maybe she had critical parents. Maybe she once had a pastor who was abusive or condemning. Who knows?

But we do know that Maria's Godview is having an increasingly dire effect on her life. You see, she's not even dating anymore. She's all but given up hope for marriage. If God doesn't want to let her experience the happiness of romantic love, why should she even try?

Maria is one of the saddest people we know.

Joshua's case is sad, too, even if he doesn't see it yet. Both of them have gotten messed up in their love life by not having an accurate view of God.

So, what *is* an accurate view of God?

In one sense, it's a mystery. We can never fully plumb the depths of God's nature and character. Quite possibly, throughout eternity to come we'll be learning more and more about God and never getting to the end of him.

In another sense, though, we *can* know who God is—the basics, anyway. The Bible gives us a broad and consistent view of him, conveying the key things we need to know. Here are three absolutely fundamental points about God for people who are seeking his will regarding marriage.

GOD IS IN CHARGE

God made the universe. He made you and us and everybody. He's the only God and Creator; everything else is his creation. He holds all authority over us and has every intention of using it. It makes sense and it's right.

But we have a way of resisting God's authority. We say we accept his sovereignty, but down deep we want to be sovereign over our own lives. We want to be free. We want to make decisions for ourselves. We want to be in charge.

Well, we've got to get over it! We need to recognize that God's authority is unlimited and submit to it. More than that—welcome it. Because God can handle being in charge. We can't.

The prophet Isaiah addressed this very conflict in our nature by referring to the practice of casting a clay pot. He posed this question (and here "clay" = us, while "potter" = God): "Does the clay say to the potter, 'What are you making?'" (Isaiah 45:9).

Well, actually, the clay might say that very thing—meaning we might foolishly presume to question what God is doing in our lives. But that isn't what we *should* be saying. Later in his prophecies, Isaiah provided the response we ought to have:

You, LORD, you are our Father. We are the clay,
you are the potter; we are all the work of your
hand.

—Isaiah 64:8

There's the right tone of acceptance and submission to the proper authority of God over our lives.

Jesus modeled this attitude when he got to the most anguishing moment of his life—praying in the Garden of Gethsemane about his impending crucifixion. He desperately wanted to avoid this unjust death and the temporary separation from his Father that it would cause. Do you remember what he prayed? "Not my will, but yours be done" (Luke 22:42).

Have you perhaps been resisting what God has done regarding your marital dreams so far in your life? Have you maybe been trying to make things happen even against what seemed to be the will of God? Look, God is not a genie existing to grant your wishes. He's the King of the universe. We're not trying to be harsh or unkind, just accurate, when we say this: whatever God chooses to do, he has the full right to do, whether it's fulfilling to you at the moment or not.

Jacob probably didn't like it when he had to wait seven years to marry Rachel (see Genesis 29). But he did it.

Not my will, but yours be done.

The lovers in the Song of Songs were feeling rather, um, urgent. But they accepted the need "not to awaken love until the time is right" (Song of Songs 2:7, NLT).

Not my will, but yours be done.

Daniel probably didn't like being made a eunuch, unable to ever marry or have children (see Isaiah 39:7). But he accepted it and lived an amazing life of faithfulness to God anyway.

Not my will, but yours be done.

Those were all real people, dealing with the same kinds of feelings we have. Their lives, and the godly principles they lived by, are instructive for us. So, we've got a radical—and unsettling—idea to try out on you: what if your love life (or lack thereof) is not primarily about your happiness but primarily about the plan of God? Think about that. And think about how real your commitment to God the King is.

GOD IS LOVING

It's important for you to remember that God Almighty is not only the sovereign ruler of the universe but he's also your loving Father. He knows your desires and loves to give you good gifts.

Yet, just as we have a way of deliberately ignoring God's authoritative Kingship, so we have a way of inadvertently forgetting his loving Fatherhood. Jesus knew this and so gave us a stunning reminder: "If you ... though you are evil, know how to give good gifts to your children, how much more will your Father in heaven give good gifts to those who ask him!" (Matthew 7:11).

We have a little daughter, Sarah. What a great kid! We love spoiling her. We love giving her gifts. And as Nicole will attest, and Brad will agree, it's Daddy who's the worst about this. He's always giving Sarah stuff she wants. When we think about God as our heavenly Father, it's all the more amazing for us to think that he wants to give *us* good things!

He wants to give you good things too. And as we have said, if you make yourself ready to receive God's best in marriage, the chances are very good that he will give such a marriage to you at just the right time. No, he's not a genie, and it's *possible* that he won't give you the kind of marriage you want, but even if that's the case, it's still all for the sake of his greater plan. He's still working out all things (even your lack of a marriage) for good to those who love him, those who have been called according to his purpose (see Romans 8:28).

Maybe you don't believe that God is a good and generous Father, wanting to give you what's good for you. Maybe you are willing to settle for okay and don't think you deserve his best. Please, think again! "Every good and perfect gift is from above, coming down from the Father of the heavenly lights" (James 1:17).

GOD KNOWS WHAT'S BEST

When our good and loving God withholds what we want (a marriage, for example), that's when we have to trust in yet one more important truth in a biblical Godview: in a targeted and personal way, God knows what's best for us.

Before marrying Brad, I (Nicole) had one boyfriend in particular who I was just sure was the right guy for me. We had so much fun together. He seemed kind and godly. I was devastated when he broke up with me on the very night (Christmas Eve) when I was sure he was going to propose. I spent months getting over the disappointment.

But do you know what? I've seen that guy go on to marry someone else, get into legal trouble with his business, get a divorce and default on his child support payments. God knew what that guy was really like; I didn't. God knew that if I married that man, my life would be filled with heartbreak. And more than that, God knew that my meeting Brad—the love of my life—was still in my future. I couldn't see it at the time, but now I'm so glad that God was watching out for me, directing me and taking care of me in accordance with his infinite knowledge. Experiences like this have helped me learn to trust him more.

Let's consider a few facts about God's knowledge.

God knows each of us perfectly.

You have searched me, LORD, and you know me. You know when I sit and when I rise; you perceive my thoughts from afar. You discern my going out and my lying down; you are familiar with all my ways.

—Psalm 139:1–3

God knows everybody else perfectly too.

From heaven the LORD looks down and sees all

mankind; from his dwelling place he watches all
who live on earth—he who forms the hearts of
all, who considers everything they do.

—Psalm 33:13–15

God knows what's coming down the road for us.

Only I can tell you the future before it even happens.

—Isaiah 46:10, NLT

In this book, we're talking about getting ready for
God's *best*. Well, we'd better recognize that only God really
understands what the best is. And only God can reliably lead us
toward it. Why, then, would we ever insist on making decisions
on our own?

YOUR GODVIEW

God is King of all, possessing the authority to do what ever he
wants. He is a loving Father who desires to give his children
good gifts. He is an all-knowing Guide through the uncertainties
of life to the best blessings he has in store. He is all these things—
and more! This is the God you must learn to know better and
better if you want to be in a position to fulfill his highest desires
for your life. His qualities will give you a balanced view of your
love life desires.

If it's true that what comes into your mind when you
think about God is the most important thing about you, then
make sure you're thinking about God as he truly is. Joshua and
Maria have failed at this so far. We want you to do better. And
we know you can, as you make sure you've got your Godview in
biblical focus.

7

HELP IS ON THE WAY

*Relying on the Holy Spirit to get you ready
for your best mate*

W e've got some bad news for you. After leading you though six chapters where we have encouraged you to be ready for God's best, it is our sad duty to inform you that you are incapable of getting yourself ready for God's best in marriage—or in any other area of your life, for that matter. You just can't do it. You don't have it in you. Sorry.

We really mean it—you're incapable of getting yourself ready. And so are we. And so is everybody else you're going to meet. However, there *is* Someone who is capable of making you ready for God's best, if you are willing to cooperate with this particular Someone. We're talking about the Holy Spirit.

Think about what God's best in marriage really means, according to the Bible (see Ephesians 5:21–33; 1 Peter 3:1–7).

If you're a man, it means you are willing to give yourself up for your wife as Christ gave himself up for the Church. You're to sanctify her, love her as you love your own body, cherish her and honor her despite her weaknesses.

If you're a woman, experiencing God's best in marriage means that you will respect your husband, honor him enough to follow his lead and cultivate the inner beauty of a gentle, quiet spirit. Do you really think you can do all this—and whatever else it might take to have the kind of marriage God wants for you—on your own? If so, good luck with that!

Friend, you need help if you are going to experience God's best in marriage. Willpower won't do it. Advice shows on TV won't do it. Your friend Ernie, who always thinks he knows best, won't do it. And reading every self-help book out there won't do it. You need the Holy Spirit to come alongside you, empower you and show you the way.

POWER SOURCE

If it's any comfort to you, the disciples of Jesus were just as much at a loss when it came to living for God as you are. When Jesus died, they hid behind locked doors. The best they could manage was to huddle together. That's why Jesus told them to wait—just hang on until he would give them what they needed. "You will receive power," he promised them, "when the Holy Spirit comes on you" (Acts 1:8).

Power. That's what the disciples needed, and that's what they got at Pentecost. Power is what you need too, if you are going to get ready for God's best. The Holy Spirit offers the power you need. And the particular kind of power we're talking about here is the *power to transform*. As you know, there are some things that need to change about you if you are going to be ready for God's best. We don't know what those things are in your particular case. You might need to overcome low self-esteem. You might need to put away immoral habits. You might need to get out of a rut and pursue the real purpose of your life. Whatever it is, we are sure that the called-for change is more than you can accomplish on your own. You need an outside power source—the Holy Spirit—to transform you.

Read Romans 7:7–25 sometime. It's the apostle Paul's remarkably vulnerable report about his own inability to do what was right. "I do not understand what I do," Paul reflected in anguish. "For what I want to do I do not do, but what I hate I do" (v. 15). Sound familiar? It was like a war was going on inside him, he said. He felt like a prisoner. It was simply a wretched experience. Still familiar?

Go on to Read Romans 8—the resolution to the problem. How was Paul able to battle through his struggle against sin? Not from fighting harder in his own personal war with himself. He needed the power of the Holy Spirit, just as we all do. The principle he discovered is this: "If you live according to the flesh, you will die; but if by the Spirit you put to death the misdeeds of the body, you will live" (v. 13).

What hope there is here! As God changes you by his Spirit, your future is changed.

We have a friend named Norm. We love Norm. We're glad to be involved in his life. But allow us to be honest with you—he used to be pretty annoying. His personality was prickly, to put it mildly. He knew it too.

What bothered Norm the most about his personality problem was that it kept hindering whatever progress he was making in his dating relationships. Women would like his looks, but as they got to know him better, his relentless tendency to become obnoxious, to tease and to get defensive turned them off. In fairness, it wasn't all his fault—he had a really difficult childhood with few good role models. But still, he had the problem to deal with.

Nevertheless, we've seen a remarkable metamorphosis in Norm over the years. We've seen him pursue a relationship with Christ and let the Holy Spirit work in him. And in the process his personality has taken on the personality of the Spirit. You know what that is, right? It's described in Galatians 5:22–23 and is made up of such qualities as love, joy, peace, patience and kindness.

The woman Norm is dating right really likes his modified personality. She thinks he's lovable. What a change!

The Holy Spirit transformed Norm by his limitless power. Wouldn't you like him to do the same for you?

Soldier recruits come out changed after they go through boot camp. Likewise, you will be changed after you experience the power of the Holy Spirit and start walking in step with him day after day. You'll be more capable. You'll achieve victory over your flaws. You'll become more winsome to others—not least of all to members of the opposite sex.

But that's not all the Spirit can do for you. He is more than just a power source for our lives. He's also a guide into the path we are supposed to take.

TRUSTWORTHY GUIDE

The disciples of Jesus knew that the Holy Spirit would be coming to them after Jesus' death and ascension to heaven. He had told them so on the night before his crucifixion. "I will ask the Father," Jesus had said, "and he will give you another advocate to be with you forever—the Spirit of truth" (John 14:16–17). We'll be looking at that interesting title "Counselor" in just a bit. But first, let's consider the other label Jesus gave to the Holy Spirit: "the Spirit of truth." The Holy Spirit is the Spirit of truth in the sense that he is filled with truth; he has no falsehood in him. But more than that, he's the Spirit of truth in the sense that he directs Christ's followers to truth.

A few minutes later in his conversation with the disciples in the upper room, Jesus circled back to the subject of the Spirit and said, "When he, the Spirit of truth, comes, he will guide you into all the truth. He will not speak on his own; he will speak only what he hears, and he will tell you what is yet to come" (John 16:13). The disciples had a unique role to fulfill in history as the transmitters of Jesus' truth to future generations. They initiated the preaching of the gospel, and some of them authored the books of the New Testament that have guided the church ever since. What they taught was true because the Holy Spirit guaranteed it, conveying truth to them straight from heaven.

But wait a minute. We were talking about marriage, not about being apostles or writing New Testament books. What does all this have to do with you?

Just this. The Holy Spirit is still the Spirit of truth. He still guides Christ's followers—not just apostles—into all truth. He'll guide *you*. And isn't guidance something you desperately need as you seek God's best for a mate?

Think about this. If you're like many people who have

been dating for a while, you've had some near misses. You've thought you'd found "the one" ... and then saw the relationship fall apart. Not only was the loss of this relationship painful to you, but you were also left wondering, *How could I have been so wrong about him (or her)?*

As you become more sensitive to the Holy Spirit, he will give you the ability to distinguish illusion from reality. You'll hear his no or his yes about whether a potential mate is right for you. This is how you'll be guided to God's best for you, sidestepping all the fair and poor options.

I (Brad) can honestly say that when Nicole and I met each other, I quickly just knew that God meant us for one another—and it was so wonderful not to be left in doubt and hesitation.

The guidance of the Holy Spirit is a blessing to cultivate in every kind of decision making as a single person and as a married one. But that's still not all we can look for from the Holy Spirit. The next blessing is the antidote to something many single people struggle with: fear.

PROTECTING HAND

Is the fear of loss or potential pain keeping you from a successful relationship? What about the fear of failure? Or the fear of repeating prior mistakes?

If that's you, you're not alone. Most of us experience those fears in the beginning of a relationship. Sometimes they are so consuming that we won't even allow ourselves to get into a new relationship. Hey, if there's no relationship, we can't mess it up, right?

What if we told you that you don't need to be ruled by fear? It's true. As the apostle Paul said, "God has not given us a spirit of fear and timidity, but of power, love, and self-discipline" (2 Timothy 1:7, NLT). How do we get rid of that spirit of fear and timidity? By letting the Holy Spirit (who is the opposite of the spirit of fear) crowd it out of our lives.

After power and guidance, the third great blessing of the

Holy Spirit is protection. As we're walking in step with him and he is directing us, we can know that he is taking care of us. It's not that we'll never suffer hurt again, but he has a way of leading Christ's followers through the worst pitfalls. Even if we do fall, he is there to pick us up again. It's not as devastating as it might have been without him leading us in our lives.

Four times Jesus referred to the Holy Spirit as the "Advocate" (John 14:16, 26; 15:26; 16:7). "Advocate" is translated from the word *paraclete*, which refers to someone who "comes alongside" someone else to bring comfort, encouragement and refreshing. Other Bible translations use the word "Helper" or "Counselor." This is what the Holy Spirit is to us. He is the person of the Trinity who comes alongside us and holds us up through the big and small challenges of life.

With him by your side, there is no reason to fear what the search for a mate will bring. You can relax and rest in him.

FILLED WITH THE HOLY SPIRIT

Guide, empower, protect. Isn't it wonderful what the Spirit does for us? But let's get practical. How can we access these blessings? Learning about what the Holy Spirit can do is not what we most want. Experiencing it is!

So there's something you need to know about: the *filling with the Holy Spirit*.

If you are a believer in Christ, you have already received the Holy Spirit. He has come to dwell within you. But that doesn't necessarily mean that you are operating in his power, guidance and protection, not to mention his other wonderful qualities. You might be operating more out of your sinful nature. And that's why, periodically, you need a new filling of the Spirit.

Ephesians 5:18 says, simply enough, "Be filled with the Spirit." This is an ongoing practice of surrendering to the Holy Spirit. To be filled with the Spirit, you simply have to let go of your resistance and give him control of your life.

Sound appealing? If you want to know if you need this filling, then here's the litmus test: Are you surrendered to the will of God or aren't you? Be honest. If you aren't surrendered to God, or aren't surrendered fully, then you need to let the Holy Spirit get behind the steering wheel of your life once again. However wonderful your relationship with him might once have been, you need to be filled with him anew—now (see Online Resources, page 201).

The late evangelist Bill Bright referred to this surrender to the Holy Spirit as "spiritual breathing." He would encourage people to "breathe out" by confessing their sin and then "breathe in" by asking the Spirit to fill and control them. It is a way of keeping close to God all the time. Try it. Talk to God. Be honest about situations where you insisted on doing things your way. Ask him for forgiveness.

> If we confess our sins, he is faithful and just and will forgive us our sins and purify us from all unrighteousness.
>
> —1 John 1:9

Then invite the Holy Spirit to once again take charge of your life as he guides you in making the choices he wants for you.

> This is the confidence that we have in approaching God: that if we ask anything according to his will, he hears us. And if we know that he hears us—whatever we ask—we know that we have what we asked of him.
>
> —1 John 5:14–15

Whenever you notice that you disobey God in some way, stop and take a moment to be filled with the Spirit again. As you are controlled by the Holy Spirit, God will guide you and bring about the changes in character necessary for successful Christian living.

You will find that the blessings of the Spirit in your life will go from showing up periodically to being a normal thing for you. You will be able to achieve what you could never achieve on your own. You'll be ready for God's best in marriage as a work of kindly grace by the Spirit. Praise God!

A SPIRIT-FILLED SPOUSE

Let us give you one last piece of advice on this subject. Don't just seek the Spirit's influence in your own life; also look for a mate who is living a Spirit-filled life.

You already know that Christians are not supposed to marry unbelievers (see 2 Corinthians 6:14–18). But that's just a minimal standard. You might have an okay marriage if that was the only standard you considered for a potential mate. But you don't want an *okay* marriage; you want a *great* marriage—God's best. And for that you need to wait for someone to marry who, like you, is walking with the Spirit.

It's a compatibility issue. If one of you is walking closely with the Spirit and one is not, you're going to experience all kinds of conflicts. But if the Holy Spirit is speaking to each of your spirits, his message will draw you together. You'll still have differences, and you may need to make adjustments from time to time, but you'll tend to have unity on essential beliefs and decisions. The Spirit will be leading you both down the same road—the road to God's highest will for your lives.

8

THE NEXT STEP

Following wherever God leads you

I (Brad) was camping once as a boy and—all by myself—had to get from a lodge to the cabin where my family was staying. It was a foggy night and pitch dark in the woods, far from civilization. My only light came from my flashlight. I vividly recall picking my way down the path. In the falling mist, my flashlight illuminated only a few feet ahead of me. I would watch my feet and try to keep from moving off the narrow dirt trail into the brush on either side. A couple of times I had to choose a fork when the trail split, but thankfully each time, as I looked up, my flashlight revealed a trail sign indicating the way I should go. It took a while, and it was sure scary for a boy of eight or nine, but by paying attention to what was ahead of me at each step, I finally made it to the cabin. How welcome the glow from the window seemed!

This is the way it is in our life with God. He doesn't show us everything at once. He doesn't give us a map laying out everything in his plan for our lives. No, he leads us bit by bit, and we have to follow one step at a time. It can be scary. It may not be how we'd like it to go, but that's why we need to trust. His Word is the "light on my path" (Psalm 119:105).

This is also the way it is for us as we search for the ideal mate. Wouldn't you like to know everything that lies ahead for your love life? When you'll meet "the one"? What you'll like about each other? How long you'll date? When you'll get engaged? When you'll get married? Well, unless you're really different from anyone else we've ever met, we don't think God is going to give you all that information in one big download. He's less interested in your engaging in long-range planning than in your committing to short-range obedience.

> In their hearts humans plan their course, but the LORD establishes their steps.
> —Proverbs 16:9

As you do the things we've already talked about—look at your life from a biblical frame of mind, see God for who he really is and rely on the Holy Spirit—you'll be more and more equipped to follow him to the wonderful destination he has for you.

THE JOURNEY VERSUS THE DESTINATION

We wonder if you've ever pondered the fact that there's a difference between *God's will* and *God's plan*. They're not contradictory; they're just not the same.

To ask, "What is God's will for me?" is to ask a destination question. In other words, where is he taking you in such-and-such an area in your life. For example, the question "What is God's will for my church involvement?" asks what church he wants you to wind up joining. It says nothing about how you'll find that church or when. Likewise, to ask, "What is God's will for my love life?" is to ask whether you'll ever be married. It doesn't address who you'll be married to, when you'll find that person or how the union will come about.

We've already said that the probability is strong that, if you get yourself ready for God's best in marriage as we're teaching you in this book, he'll give it to you. That's God's will for you in that area of your life. But it's not God's plan.

You see, to ask, "What is God's plan for me?" is to ask a journey question. It covers all of the when, where, how and who issues. So, if you're looking for a new church, his *will* for you might be to attend First Community Church. But his *plan* for you might be to visit a number of other churches first, meet a new friend who is a member at First Community and not attend your first service at your new church until next year. And similarly, even though his *will* is for you to be married, ahead of you still lies a whole process of undergoing personal change, looking for the right mate, getting to know that person and moving toward marriage together. That's his *plan*, and you don't know what it looks like yet.

It's easy to get God's will and his plan mixed up, isn't it? We can even see it in the Bible. For example, David knew it was God's will to build a temple. But God had to explain to David that it was his plan to build the temple at a later time, using David's son Solomon and not David himself as the builder (see 1 Kings 8:17-19). But in this respect, you're better off than David was, because now you know the difference between God's will and his plan and you can act accordingly.

God's plan requires you to trust and obey. He'll let you know his *will* for you in advance, but he'll only reveal his *plan* step by step. We're back to the flashlight illuminating one piece of the trail at a time. Take the step in front of you and don't worry about all the twists and turns that lie out of sight. God knows what he's doing.

GOD'S HIGHER THOUGHTS

The reason we have a hard time giving up our headlong pursuit of our own plan in favor of following God's plan step by step is that our plan makes sense to us. When a young man becomes infatuated with a young woman, for example, it may make total sense to him to pursue her romantically with everything he's got and rush toward marriage with her. He thinks he's being logical, even wise, about this. It never occurs to him to slow down and try to figure out what God would have him do in this situation.

Like that young man, we have a problem with holding too high an opinion of our own ability to understand what's going on around us and to reason things out for ourselves. This is true in every area of life, but it's especially true in matters of the heart, when intense feelings can cloud our judgment.

And that's why we need to cultivate a trust in God's superior understanding. Our reasoning is natural and flawed. His reason is supernatural and perfect. As the prophet Isaiah said, God's thinking operates on an entirely different level from ours.

> "My thoughts are not your thoughts, neither are your ways my ways," declares the LORD, "As the heavens are higher than the earth, so are my ways higher than your ways and my thoughts than your thoughts."
>
> —Isaiah 55:8–9

The simple fact is that God's ways aren't natural to us. They are mysterious. He is a God of surprises. Take the issue of timing, for example. When there's something we want (say, a wonderful marriage), when do we want it? *Now!* But God is looking at the bigger picture, seeing all the things that go into it. He wants us to have a wonderful marriage too, but it might not be right now. He's got good reasons for some other timing, and we just have to trust his thinking on that.

We're not trying to get you to stop reasoning for yourself; we're just trying to get you to adopt *sanctified* reasoning—reasoning that's shaped and guided by God. We believe this is biblical. When Proverbs 3:5 says, "lean not on your own understanding," it's not saying to stop using your mind. It's saying to stop relying on your natural thinking and start cultivating your supernatural thinking. As we learned in the previous chapter, the Holy Spirit guides our thinking. He helps us to reason through Scripture and thus understand our own situation better. The result is that, rather than being mindless, "we have the mind of Christ" (1 Corinthians 2:16).

When we begin to take on the mind of Christ, and accept the fact that God knows better than we do, then it becomes easier to trust him as he escorts us along the journey to his best for us.

TRUSTWORTHY

I (Nicole) remember attending a party at a friend's house once when I was seventeen. I didn't get my driver's license until the following year, so my mother had dropped me off at the party. But the party wasn't going to break up until 11:00 p.m. or so, and my mom didn't want to come out that late at night to pick me up. I was supposed to get a ride home with someone from the party.

As my mother had asked, I called her when I was ready to come home, and our phone conversation went something like this:

"Hi, Mom. I'm ready to come home. See you soon."

"Wait a minute, Nicole. Who's driving you?"

"A girl named Megan. You don't know her. She's Stephanie's friend."

"She has a driver's license, right? What's she driving?"

"Sure, she's got a license, Mom. She's a senior. She's driving her folks' car."

"Did you tell her how far out of town we live? She doesn't mind coming out here?"

"I told her, Mom. She doesn't have to be home until midnight, so she's got time. Relax. I better go."

"Not yet you don't, young lady. Has this girl been drinking or doing drugs? I want the truth."

"No, Mom! She hasn't had a thing to drink. Neither have I. Come on."

"All right, honey, I believe you. You go get your ride and I'll see you soon."

My mom's questioning annoyed me at the time (moms *always* annoy their teenage daughters), but since then I have thought about the conversation and have come to appreciate what she was doing. Consider this: My mom was trying to determine …

- if Megan, my volunteer driver, had the *ability* to get me home (had a car and a driver's license)

81

- if she had the *willingness* to drive me home (didn't mind taking me so far)
- if she had the *integrity* to get me safely home (was sober)

And do you know what? Not only was Mom being a responsible parent by asking these questions, but she was also (unknown to her) giving us some questions we can use to reassure ourselves about trusting God with our love life—and everything else that's precious to us, for that matter.

Does God have the ability to lead us to the ideal mate for us? Sure, he does! He's Almighty God. He knows us, knows the other person and is fully capable of orchestrating events to put us together as we follow his lead.

> Ah, Sovereign LORD, you have made the heavens and the earth by your great power and outstretched arm. Nothing is too hard for you.
> —Jeremiah 32:17

Does God have the willingness to put us together with our intended mate? Again, sure! As we saw in chapter 1, he's a loving Father who desires to give good gifts. Unless there is something unusual in his plan for our lives, marriage is a part of it.

> The LORD's unfailing love surrounds the one who trusts in him.
> —Psalm 32:10

And finally, does God have the integrity we need to see in order of us to trust him for a spouse? Absolutely. His faithfulness is unmatched. He fulfills every promise he ever makes.

> Let us hold tightly without wavering to the hope we affirm, for God can be trusted to keep his promise.
> —Hebrews 10:23, NLT

With all this in mind, as I said to my mom on the phone those years ago, relax! Even if right now all you can see ahead of you is one step toward receiving God's best for you in marriage, you can trust him for the entire journey.

THE DEMONSTRATION OF TRUST

Would you say that you trust God? If your answer is yes, then let us ask you this: are your actions bearing out your claim?

You see, real trust is not lip service or mere feelings. There must be substance behind it. There must be obedience as a demonstration of our trust. We're not talking about taking a leap off a bridge, mind you. But we are talking about taking a step of faith. Just one. And then another, and another …

We don't know what the next step for you might be. God may be leading you to accept a blind date your friend wants to set up for you. He might want you to join an online dating community. He might want you to get back in touch with an old flame. But whatever it is, *that's* what you should do now.

It's true that the journey ahead of you might be longer than you wish. You may go through dark valleys. There might be detours and there might be drop-offs on either side. Whatever the case may be, it's okay. If you just do the next step, you will get there.

Are you feeling nervous right now? Discouraged, even? Trust that God hasn't forgotten you. He's right there with you—listening to you, loving you, desiring a closer relationship with you. Lean on his Word and his understanding in times of seeming hopelessness, and he will provide you with the love, strength and encouragement you need to take the next step.

BUILDING ON THE FOUNDATION

In part 2 of this book we have taken you on what may at times have felt like a roundabout journey to the goal of finding your soul mate. Let's take a moment to review what we've learned so far. If we want God's best in marriage, we must make sure that we …

- know God and follow him faithfully (chapter 4)
- hold to beliefs that are consistent with the Bible (chapter 5)
- see God as he really is (chapter 6)
- are filled with the Holy Spirit (chapter 7)
- trust and obey God step by step (chapter 8)

Big stuff, huh? Important stuff. As a matter of fact, all of the areas we've covered are foundational to the kind of spiritual transformation that will serve you well in every part of life. And we assure you that that includes your search for a soul mate.

With the principles of part 2 under your belt, you now have the spiritual processes in place to reason through what we're getting into in part 3. It's time to unload your baggage.

PART 3

UNLOAD
YOUR BAGGAGE

9

WRONG MOTIVES

Having the right reasons for wanting to marry

One day, as part of an exercise we were doing with the singles group we lead, we asked the thirty or so men and women in the group to write down their reasons for wanting to get married. Have you ever really thought about *why* you want to get married? Maybe you have. But we've observed that a lot of single people never articulate to themselves the reasons behind their longing to marry. And we thought that it would be helpful to encourage our group members to examine their motivations.

Here is a sampling of responses from the slips of paper they returned to us:

- "I get so lonely being all by myself so much of the time."
- "I just love being in love, having someone to be with on special occasions and to show me that I'm his number one."
- "I feel I have so much to give but nobody to give it to."
- "I want some big, strong arms around me."
- "This might sound silly, but I'm embarrassed to be single around my married friends."
- "I could use some you-know-what."
- And then there's the classic "I can't cook." (The responses were anonymous, but we're pretty sure we

know the guy who wrote that one!)

We think these responses more or less span the usual gamut of motivations for wanting to get married. We might label them like this:

- Companionship—wanting to share life with someone else.
- Romance—wanting the excitement of love.
- Care-giving—wanting to meet the needs of someone else.
- Security—wanting someone else to protect and provide for you.
- Self-esteem—wanting others to know you can get a spouse.
- Sex—wanting, well … "you-know-what."
- Practicality—wanting help with daily needs.

Most people probably have not just one but a combination of these motivations for wanting to marry. One motivation may predominate over another at any given time. Which motives rise to the top for you?

Consider this: It's not just which motives you have but also what you're doing with them.

GOOD MOTIVES GONE BAD

All of the motives we've just looked at can be good or they can be bad, depending on how we approach them. To illustrate, let us tell you about a single friend of ours—Jenny—who is big on what might be considered the most altruistic of these motives: care-giving.

Have you ever heard the old Jefferson Airplane song that includes these lines?

Don't you want somebody to love?
Don't you need somebody to love?
Wouldn't you love somebody to love?
You better find somebody to love.

That could be Jenny's theme song. She *needs* somebody to love. She's a giving person, a thoughtful person. She wants a husband so that she can lavish on him all the love and care that's inside her.

What could be wrong with that, right? After all, wanting to give love is a part of being made in the image of God. It's in his nature to generously share his love. He's made us to experience that love, to return it to him and then to turn around and share it with others as well (see 1 John 4:19). You might even speculate that the reason some single people dote on their pets so much is that, in the absence of a spouse, they need someone to become the object of their love and care.

Care-giving is a good thing, but any good thing can go wrong. Take Jenny's case. She has a way of finding boyfriends who are needy and messed up and then trying to fix them. For example, there was the one who was just downright lazy and wouldn't work. But Jenny sympathized with every story he fed her about how he had been mistreated. She made excuses for him and gave him money for rent and car repairs. What he needed was a kick in the pants! He was using her, but she'd developed a kind of messiah complex that was taking her laudable tendency to care for others and making her a victim. Meeting genuine needs in a generous way is one thing; enabling unhealthy desires in a codependent way is something else entirely.

That's how the good/bad options work for care-giving. Something similar happens with every other motivation too.

It's good to want companionship (see Genesis 2:18). Who doesn't want someone to spend life with? But what if you're selfish and you just want someone to do what you want to do, without regard to his or her interests? That's bad.

It's good to want romance—the attraction of two people for each other (see Song of Solomon). But some people want romance for its own sake, for how it makes them feel. The reality of the other person doesn't matter as much to them, and that's bad.

It's good to want security, too. Perhaps women, in

particular, tend to have a desire for someone to protect them. But if a woman were to get married to a man just because he's rich or strong and can take care of her, that would be bad.

It's good to have a healthy self-image and seek appropriate respect from others, but does it really make sense to be embarrassed by the state of singleness God has you in right now? That's being too sensitive and it's bad.

It's good to desire sex within marriage (see 1 Corinthians 7:9). But as everyone knows, sex is one of the most easily distorted gifts that God has given us. Misguided impatience for sex, then, is bad.

It's good to want practical help, too (see Ecclesiastes 4:9–12). A man might want a wife who will take care of the home, or a woman might want a husband who will take the car into the shop. But entering into a marriage just for what you can get out of it is bad.

Whenever our motives for marriage become tainted, there's one problem at the root: selfishness. So after we ask ourselves the question *What are my motives for marriage?* we also have to ask ourselves, *Are my motives tainted by selfishness?*

GOD'S MOTIVES FOR OUR MARRIAGE

We've discussed why singles are looking for a marriage partner. But what are *God's* reasons for human marriage? Have you ever asked yourself that? It's even more important than evaluating one's own motivation.

We would like to suggest three reasons God has for calling his children into marriage.

To make us holy

Author Gary Thomas wrote a book called Sacred Marriage that has an interesting subtitle. The subtitle asks, "What if God designed marriage to make us holy instead of happy?"

Well, we think it's both: God wants us to be holy *and* happy in marriage. But Thomas is right in that the worldly viewpoint of marriage is just to increase one's personal happiness, and that is selfish. We need to be mindful that there is an often-overlooked spiritual reason for marriage and it is to become more fully transformed into the image of Christ.

In marriage we learn how to give ourselves to another, as Christ gave himself for us. As we experience life from the close encounters of matrimony, marriage becomes a spotlight that exposes our flaws and sins so that we can open ourselves to the Spirit's purifying influence.

To make us more effective in his service

The apostle Paul wrote repeatedly about the church as a unity that the Holy Spirit puts together, each member bringing complementary spiritual gifts to the whole for greater effectiveness.

In this sense, marriage is a little like a church. The husband and wife each bring different experiences, interests and abilities to the marriage, making them more effective for his service together than either could be individually.

Before we were married, my (Brad's) finances were a mess. I wasn't good with numbers or details and so I was a terrible money manager, wasting my resources and always getting confused over my accounts. When I married Nicole, I gladly turned over management of the household accounts to her. She's efficient and clear-headed. And as a result, our finances are now on solid ground, making it possible for us to not only pay our bills but also give regularly to the Lord's work. I feel like I'm finally being a good steward of my finances—because of Nicole.

That's just one little example of how being married can make two people better able to serve. We've known other couples who have worked together to lead mission teams, counsel engaged couples, take in foster children and do much more that neither could have done so well alone.

To represent him to the world

In Paul's well-known writing about marriage in Ephesians 5, he quotes Genesis 2:24 about two becoming one in marriage (see v.31) and then goes on to say, "This is a profound mystery—but I am talking about Christ and the Church" (v.32).

Marriage between a man and a woman is a little picture of the "marriage" between the Bride of Christ (the Church) and the great Bridegroom (Christ). It's an image of unity with loving self-sacrifice on one side and loving devotion on the other. No other relationship in the universe comes nearly so close as marriage does to reflecting believers' union with the Lord.

At its best, then, godly marriage is a kind of witness to unbelievers—and a reminder to believers—of what kind of relationship we're supposed to have with God.

Making us holy, making us more effective, representing him. Besides these three, there are no doubt other reasons that God has for marriage. Certainly one reason would be to bear and raise children (see Genesis 1:28). But the three reasons we've focused on are sufficient to show the profoundly spiritual purpose behind marriage.

Before we go further, we want to be clear on one thing: we are *not* saying that single people cannot be holy, cannot be effective for God or cannot represent him well. We *are* saying that marriage offers different and important ways to achieve these spiritual goals, and we need to take these goals into account when we look at why and how we are pursuing a soul mate.

SELF-EVALUATION

Let's go back to why we're looking at motives for marriage in the first place. If we want to be the right kind of person who will attract the right person to us, we need to have the right motives for wanting to be married in the first place.

Consider an amazing passage from the New Testament, and we think it will all come together for you.

> You desire but do not have, so you kill. You covet but you cannot get what you want, so you quarrel and fight. You do not have because you do not ask God. When you ask, you do not receive,

because you ask with wrong motives, that you
may spend what you get on your pleasures.
—James 4:2–3

Store that passage in your mind as we ask you a couple
of questions: Have you been praying for a mate and not getting
what you ask for? If so, what has that "No" to your prayers done
to you?

We've known people who were so intent on getting the
marriage of their desires that they have done things they never
should have. Things like tell lies, manipulate others and dress
seductively. And things even worse than that. We've known men
who have broken up marriages because they wanted someone
else's wife for themselves. We've known women who have gotten
pregnant to trap a guy into marriage.

It's not pleasant to discuss these things, but they're real,
aren't they? They're what people can get into when they allow
themselves to be overcome by their sinful desires. This is what
happens when motives that were once pure become severely
tainted.

We hope you've never gotten into a situation like this. But
quite possibly you are feeling frustrated, maybe even angry at
God, because your request for a marriage has gone unanswered
so far. If so, that's why we've been forcing you to face your motives in this chapter. If the problem isn't that you've failed to pray
for what you want, then perhaps "you do not receive, because
you ask with wrong motives."

Let us give you an assignment. Set aside some time (maybe right now) and get in an attitude of prayer. Ask God to reveal
to you by his Holy Spirit if any of your motives for marriage are
self-centered or wrong. Then listen to him. Confess sin, if you
need to. Embrace God's reasons for marriage and be ready to
return to your search for a soul mate with purified motives in
your heart.

Be encouraged! You've just taken a big step toward
becoming the right person for the right person for you.

10

RELATIONSHIP IDOLATRY

Keeping God at the center of your life

What does the word *idol* mean to you? A reality show featuring ambitious singers? Aspirations to achieve the status of a favorite athlete, actress or writer? Exotic trinkets that supposedly bring either good or "taboo" to their bearers, depending on the whims of the "god" or "gods" they represent? If you're familiar with the Old Testament or ancient religions, maybe you think of statues that people would offer sacrifices to in the old days.

For Christians, it's easy to restrict the perception of an idol to a blatant act of sin, such as the one found in Exodus 32. True, we may not hoist an actual golden calf aloft and bow down before it, but idol worship is alive and well in our culture. Today the sin of idolatry tends to be insidious, creeping bit by bit into our lives and replacing Christ with a worldly "savior."

For single believers in particular, one major idol can be something that, in and of itself, is holy and ordained by God himself: the desire for marriage with a soul mate. Of course, there is nothing wrong with seeking a godly spouse to love, honor and cherish until death do you part. Nor is there anything inherently sinful about picturing a dream wedding or the (seemingly) perfect spouse to take home after that celebratory night. None of these things are sinful per se. A marriage that honors Christ is both holy and beautiful. After all, God himself stated in

Genesis that it is "not good" for man to be alone (see 2:18), and he created Eve.

But at what point do we cross the line and become engaged (pardon the pun) in the all-consuming sin of idolatry? The key word here is "all-consuming." God stated plainly:

> "You must not have any other god but me. You must not make for yourself an idol of any kind or an image of anything in the heavens or on the earth or in the sea. You must not bow down to them or worship them, for I, the LORD your God, am a jealous God who will not tolerate your affection for any other gods."
>
> —Exodus 20:3–5, NLT

WHEN YOUR SEARCH BECOMES ALL-CONSUMING

In simplistic terms, an idol represents any object that knocks the real God off the throne in favor of a false god.

Let us return to Jenny, the young woman we introduced in the last chapter. She felt a deep need to be loved, and it led her to do too much for needy boyfriends. I (Nicole) informally counseled Jenny to try to figure out what was going on inside her and help her learn to seek God's best instead of the world's second best.

We were at a coffee shop one day when I asked Jenny how she spent her time.

"Well, after work, I sometimes go out with some of the single crowd from my building to get a drink or eat out," Jenny said. "Believe it or not, there are some great-looking guys at my accounting firm!"

She went on. "At home I get bored, so I usually check a couple apps on my phone that let me talk anonymously with local guys I haven't met in person. It might sound weird to you, but these things have led to some dates when I really liked how the guy communicated online."

I nodded to keep Jenny talking. "Also," Jenny said, "I go to a lot of parties on the weekends."

"Because of the guys, again?" I asked.

"Sure!" Jenny laughed. "Yeah, I know some of the guys I've dated have kind of used me at times. But that's okay. I'm not giving up."

"How often do you go to church? Are you in a Bible study group? Do you have a routine for devotions?" I probed.

"I go to events for the singles groups at your church and at two other churches in town. I don't really have time for a Bible study or devotions."

She looked me straight in the eyes and said, "I know you probably think I'm too focused on going out with guys. But being single, I'm telling you, I feel like I'm not living yet. Sometimes it seems to me like adult life isn't even going to really start until I'm married. Then I'll have a real purpose and something to focus on. So right now, I've just got to get a husband!"

As much as I could sympathize with Jenny's loneliness, and as high a view of marriage as I have, I *was* worried about how much importance Jenny was putting on getting married. It was clearly something Jenny was thinking about and pursuing in every way she could whenever she could. I imagined that God, up in heaven, wished he received half as much attention from Jenny as she gave to the search for a husband!

KEEPING YOUR RELATIONSHIP WITH GOD YOUR NUMBER ONE PRIORITY

Can you relate at all to Jenny? How much of your mind, your time and or your heart is consumed with worshiping the search for a soul mate?

If your honest evaluation leads you to believe you might be tipping the scales toward idolatry, you will need to put things back into the proper biblical perspective. First, repent and restore God to his proper place in your life. Pray that God will help you resist the temptation to focus too much of your time and energy on the search for a spouse. Ask him to fill you with a desire for things that are honoring to him, including serving him and reading his Word. It may be helpful to make (or renew) a dedication of your body to the Lord, as Paul says:

> I urge you, brothers and sisters, in view of God's mercy, to offer your bodies as a living sacrifice, holy and pleasing to God—this is your true and proper worship. Do not conform to the pattern of this world, but be transformed by the renewing of your mind. Then you will be able to test and approve what God's will is—his good, pleasing and perfect will.
>
> —Romans 12:1–2

Second, we need to remember that, as Christians, we are God's vessels—created to manifest his goodness in all we do, whether married or single. How are we honoring God if we spend our days worshipping at the altar of self (the root of idolatry)? Is your desire for marriage and your quest for a soul mate quenching the Holy Spirit's work in your life? Remember that a mate is a gift and God is the Giver.

Finally, we must remember that, before we ever become engaged to an earthly mate, we are already betrothed to the Bridegroom, who is Christ (see Ephesians 5:25–27). Imagine how disrespectful it would be for a bride to walk down the church aisle with her eyes darting around at the flowers or the stained-glass windows, admiring everything but her future spouse. Yet such a tragedy becomes reality when we focus more on our quest for a mate than on a relationship with our heavenly Beloved.

For us as Christians, the deep hole of loneliness we may feel within while we are single is God-shaped, not ring-shaped, and can only be filled by him, not by a mate, no matter how ideal that mate might be. A marriage partner can never take the place of God in our lives. Walking down the aisle, taking sacred vows and sailing off into the sunset with another imperfect, sinful being can never truly fulfill us the way a relationship with a perfect and holy God can.

This is a short chapter, but the principle is important: Do not let your *desire* for a soul mate take the place of your *relationship* with God.

11

UNHEALTHY BEHAVIOR

Learning from the past to prepare for the future

This is the chapter we could hardly wait to write—and can hardly wait for you to read. Not that the other chapters are not important too, but this chapter is really important when it comes to unloading sin habits that will jeopardize your future.

Experiences from our past, whether positive or negative, can have a strong effect on our lives and our behavior. Great experiences can give us confidence and faith. But sometimes bad experiences can make us bitter, fearful and untrusting and can produce a devastating effect on our lives and our relationships.

The good news is that negative experiences can be turned into positives for our future if we let God heal us and teach us what we should learn from them—allowing him to conform us to the character of Christ.

GETTING HEALTHY

You may never have been married before. You may never have even had a serious romantic relationship. But you certainly have had relationships of many kinds (family relationships, friendships, work relationships), and your history with other people has established certain patterns in your behavior. Our goal is to help you look at these patterns and make changes where you need to.

We want you to be relationship ready, so that as soon as God brings your ideal mate into your life you'll be prepared to receive the gift. And then you won't have to backtrack in the midst of your marriage to correct your harmful patterns. You'll thank us later if you heed our advice now.

Think of it this way. When you've got a sloppy, messy cold—with lots of sneezing and nose blowing—is it fun to kiss your boyfriend or girlfriend? Well, maybe, kind of, for a while. But not as much fun for either of you as it is when you are healthy. (And besides, if you do kiss, your girlfriend or boyfriend will probably come down with the same cold!)

It's the same way if your behavior is unhealthy. The last thing you want to do is to get into a relationship with a person who has wonderful potential as a mate while you're still sick. Get healthy first—cooperate with God to change your behavior pattern—and then be ready to take advantage of what God is bringing to you.

VICES REPLACED WITH VIRTUES

Heather turns off men with her bitter and sarcastic attitude.

Julio indulges in Internet porn.

Tracy annoys her roommates with her messiness and a tendency to lose things.

Ivan has racked up huge credit card bills through buying the latest toys and gadgets.

Farah is way too quick to share the intimate details of her heart.

We've changed the names, but these are all real problems we've dealt with among the single people in the group we work with at our church. And we could easily extend the list across the next couple of pages. We know that some of these things might seem like mere personal quirks, but we prefer to use an old-fashioned term for them: *vices*. They are habits of bad behavior.

You might think that the answer to vices is simply to eliminate them. Heather needs to get rid of the bitterness. Julio needs to quit with the porn. And so on. True enough—as far as it goes. But eliminating vices is only half the answer, and maybe not even the most important half. Installing virtues in their place is the other half. In fact, we'd argue that it's usually *impossible* to permanently eliminate a vice without putting a virtue in its place. Heather needs to stop being bitter—*and* develop a warmhearted attitude toward men. Julio needs to stop viewing porn—*and* achieve a sexual purity that tears down barriers between himself and others.

Sounds good, right? "But how?" you might ask.

YOUR SOUL PRESCRIPTION

We like the process outlined by Bill Bright and Henry Brandt in their book *Soul Prescription*. Bright and Brandt propose five steps that can take anyone from vice to virtue in the areas that are problems for them. We suggest that you spend some time doing a prayerful self-evaluation to identify areas where you've developed habits that could threaten your upcoming God's-best relationship. Ask God to reveal these vices to you. Ask close friends to give you an honest appraisal too. And then think it all through yourself, humbly and honestly. Finally work through the five *Soul Prescription* steps for each of these areas in your life. We believe they can revolutionize your life and make you relationship ready.

1. Adopt a correct view of God.

Surprise! You're already further along in this process than you think. Without your even knowing it, we gave you a head start with chapter 6. Remember the quote from A. W. Tozer? "What comes into our minds when we think about God is the most important thing about us." Throughout chapter 6 we explored the importance of having a proper Godview.

As you focus on mistakes in your past relationships, think about how a flawed view of God may lie behind your behavior. For example, if former boyfriends complained that you didn't show them enough respect, is it possible you have failed to keep in mind that God is the One who made human beings in his image and redeemed them at the cost of his Son's life? God has given all people an inherent dignity, and you should be recognizing it in your relationships.

Whatever the vices you're hoping to root out, trace their

origin back to possible problems in your view of God. Keep on striving to know him better and better.

2. Revise your false beliefs.

People can have warped ideas about God—but that's not all. They can also have warped ideas about themselves, other people and how life works. When this happens, then (as we said in chapter 5) they need the Bible to transform their thinking.

We worked with one young woman—we'll call her Tina—who tended to be secretive and even deceitful. She wouldn't share much of anything about herself even with people who were trying to befriend her in our singles group. She would tell little lies about herself so that people wouldn't know what she was really like.

This behavior seemed really odd to us at first. But as we got to know Tina better, little by little we found out that she had been hurt rather badly by people in the past. She was trying to protect herself by hiding and lying. Obviously this pattern didn't bode well for any future marriage she might have, since transparency with one's mate is a key to success in marriage.

Tina had a false belief: *People aren't trustworthy. Therefore, I can't open up to anyone.* Slowly she is beginning to see that some relationships really are safe places. She can share her heart with others. We're hoping that, as she shares the truth about herself with friends, she's developing skills that will serve her well in marriage.

She's revising her false beliefs. Where do you need to do the same?

3. Repent of your sin.

Language provides all kinds of euphemisms for our wrongdoing—*mistake, goof, indiscretion* and so on. The Bible, however, provides an ugly (but truthful) little word: *sin.* This word reminds us that we didn't just commit an unfortunate misstep; we trespassed against the laws of Almighty God. As we look back on our behavior in past relationships, all of us have to admit that we've committed our share of sins.

That's why repentance is step three—the turning point—in the *Soul Prescription* process. We have to go to God, confess our sins, ask his forgiveness and receive his cleansing. This is the only way to achieve the turnaround we really need in our life. It's the decisive act that pushes away the errors of the past and opens space for what God wants to do in us in the future.

Our friend Megan had a habit of acting in an excessively flirty way. She didn't even realize she was doing it until a couple of her friends confronted her about it. She was appalled. And she did the right thing: she told God she was sorry and asked for forgiveness. That became a decisive turning point for her in her behavior with men.

Want a clean break with your sins and vices of the past so that your new relationship can be a healthy one? You must repent. Don't delay. Do it at once.

4. Defend against spiritual attacks.

Many Christians think that repenting of sin is the end of the story. If only that were true! If we have repented, we can be sure that we are forgiven (1 John 1:9), but that doesn't mean the temptations are over.

The Bible tells us about three enemies of holiness:
- The world—values that contradict the values of God
- The flesh—sinful desires that trouble us as Christians
- The devil—a spiritual adversary who employs
  schemes to entice us into doing wrong

Each of these is a serious enemy, but none of them is as fearsome as we might think. Jesus said he has "overcome the world" (John 16:33). Paul said, "You have no obligation to do what your sinful nature [flesh] urges you to do" (Romans 8:12, NLT). And the apostle James said, "Resist the devil, and he will flee from you" (James 4:7).

If our friend Ivan were to break down his problem with overspending, he might discover this: The world is telling him that he deserves to buy what he wants even if he has to stretch his credit to the limit. The flesh is telling him that he just has to have the experience of the latest stuff. And the devil is whispering, "It's no big deal if you don't have the money for it. Go ahead and get it."

These three opponents play on the same team, and they've always got something in their playbook for us.

Expect spiritual attack, but also be strong in faith to resist and hold to your new course.

5. Flee temptation.

You don't have to just stand in readiness waiting for spiritual attack; you can also take practical steps to remove yourself from temptation. We recommend these steps: Spend more time with God, filling your mind with thoughts of him. Go to the Bible and memorize promises that you can hold on to when you are tempted. Seek accountability with trusted Christian friends and otherwise establish safeguards to maintain your new holiness.

We give credit to Julio for buying filtering software that will prevent him from accessing pornographic websites on his computer and his phone. He's getting help wherever he can. He's determined. He wants purity—and he's going to get it!

Likewise, with your own safeguards in place, you can do more than just hope for a transition from vice to virtue. You can be confident of it. You can pursue victory and *expect* it. Thanks be to God!

Please take the five steps from *Soul Prescription* seriously. They have the power to affect a permanent change in your character (see Online Resources, page 201).

Remember, God gives generously of his grace. He wants to change you for the better more than you want to be changed. Although you may have had a part in a relationship breakup and you might feel like you don't deserve anything good, God still has grace for you. He can replace sinful qualities in you with Spirit-filled character qualities.

Pursue a soul-deep correction from your failures of the past. And while you're doing it, look for someone to marry who has also dealt with the past failures in his or her life. When two healthy people come together in God's will and marry, their marriage can hardly fail to be healthy too.

DEALING WITH PAST HURTS

I (Nicole) would like to conclude this chapter by speaking from my heart to your heart. You see, I know what it's like to be hurt in a romantic relationship. It happened to me—more than once.

The incident that stands out the most in my mind happened with a boyfriend named Darren. I was twenty-four, and ours was a whirlwind romance, from blind date to engagement ring in nine weeks. One day I had just gotten back from the bridal store with my beautiful new wedding gown when Darren showed up unexpectedly at my door. I hurriedly hung the gown in my closet and couldn't wait to talk to him. But in moments, everything I was dreaming about changed.

He'd begun to have second thoughts about us, he said. We'd rushed into things. It wasn't me; he wasn't sure he wanted to get married to anyone yet. He wanted a break from seeing me.

Apart from a few phone calls, I never saw or heard from him again.

That wedding dress hung in my closet for years. I could have done something else with it, but it was almost like I wanted something to remind myself of my breakup as often as I opened my closet door. For years the dress hung there, and for years I grieved the loss of my engagement and the lack of a husband in my life. How many times I cried over that dress!

Did I wear that dress when I married Brad, you wonder? I thought about it. It could have been a symbol of triumph, I suppose. But no, I deliberately got rid of that dress and bought another one for my wedding with Brad. I'd found God's best for me. I was done with both my past hurts and my past wedding gown. The new lay before me.

I tell you all this because I want you to know that you can get past not only the *sin* involved in past relationships but also the *pain*. You can do more than get out of a rut; you can also give up your baggage. The God who made your emotions knows how you're hurting from former mistreatment and how that holdover from the past is hobbling you in the present. When you cry, he cries alongside you. And I promise—*I promise*—that he is at work even now to bring healing and recovery to your precious heart.

> He heals the brokenhearted and binds up their wounds.
>
> —Psalm 147:3

New life even now is sprouting in the burned-over field of your heart, and soon you will have a meadow of beautiful flowers there to offer the mate God will escort into your life. Learn to overcome negatives from your past and live the life God desires for you.

12

POOR DECISION-MAKING

Following godly wisdom as you proceed toward God's best for you

There are so many decisions we make involved in romantic relationships.

> *She's cute and she seems nice. Should I ask her out?*
>
> *Should I say "I love you" to him?*
>
> *Have we reached a stage where it's safe for me to share the junk from my past?*
>
> *Should we move toward engagement, or is this just a dating relationship that's run its course?*
>
> *We got engaged—that's amazing! But what else do we need to do to make sure our marriage gets off to a good start?*

How do you make these kinds of decisions?

In this book so far, we've talked about many aspects of getting ready for God's best in a mate. But before you move on from *getting ready* for God's best to actually *finding* God's best, we think there's one more skill you ought to learn: how to make wise and godly decisions that will affect your future happiness in marriage.

We said earlier that there's a difference between God's will and God's plan. You may be certain that God has called you to be married. If so, that's his *will* for you. But his *plan* for how to get you there is different. And it's going to involve a lot of decision-making along the way.

Most people don't really think about how they make

decisions. But it's really important. Even if you don't have a decision to make regarding your love life right now, someday you will. We want to help you decide how to decide.

THE ACTOR AND THE ENGINEER

We know a fellow named Damien who has a totally "out there" personality. He's emotional. He's extroverted. He's demonstrative. He's also an actor—that explains a lot! Whenever Damien has a decision to make, he "goes with his gut," as he himself puts it. Since he's got such an acute intuition, his "gut" often makes quite a good decision. But we've also known him to get into some things that made us wonder, *What was he thinking?* That's the problem. He *wasn't* thinking.

Damien is dating a girl who is his opposite in many ways, including how she makes decisions. The contrast between them is a source of considerable amusement to us. Veronica is a chemical engineer by profession, and she is all about logic and reasoning. When she's got a decision to make, she takes her time and gathers all the information she can, then she sorts through it analytically. We've even known her to make charts with all the pros and cons related to a particular decision side by side. How different from Damien!

The truth is, we all have a typical style of decision-making. And in any given situation, each of us might go overboard with feelings or thinking as we try to make a decision, just as Damien and Veronica are inclined to do. But we need to realize that we can change the way we make choices.

So, how does a person make wise choices?

Balance head and heart. Is that what you were expecting us to say? Wrong! Combining intuition and analysis might be helpful, but we've got a more powerful suggestion for you. What would you think about not merely combining head and heart but raising both of them from the natural level to the supernatural level?

SANCTIFIED FEELING AND SANCTIFIED REASONING

Just because you're analytical doesn't mean you're thinking in a godly way. And just because you're intuitive doesn't mean you're tuned in to the promptings of the Holy Spirit.

A long time ago, something really bad happened called the Fall. People ever since Adam and Eve have been tainted by sin, like a drop of blue food coloring staining a whole cup of water pale blue. Our heart and head were not immune to these effects. Our mind is fallen and our emotions are too.

Even for those of us who have been saved by Jesus Christ and are indwelled by the Holy Spirit, we're still fighting our own sinful natures. At times we can engage in unsanctified reasoning and indulge in unsanctified feeling. God isn't directing those thoughts or inspiring those emotions, so if we let ourselves be guided by them, we can easily go astray.

But it doesn't have to be that way. Your mind can be renewed (see Romans 12:2), and your heart can be too (see Ezekiel 36:26). We've got a process that will help.

HOW TO MAKE HOLY CHOICES

The website myPraize.com offers a step-by-step plan for discerning God's will that we really like (see Online Resources, page 201). It's not that this is the *only* way to discern God's will or that you must always follow every single step, but what we like about it is that it combines both heart and head in a way that subjects both to the wisdom of God. After all, you want to know *God's* desires regarding the decisions you must make in finding *God's* best. Here's how.

Step 1. Define your situation.

Do you need to decide if the first date went well enough to try for a second date? Are you wondering what is appropriate physical touch in your relationship? Do you have some worries about compatibility with your boyfriend or girlfriend? Whatever your situation is, make sure you've clearly defined it for yourself so that you can specifically seek God's will in the matter.

Damien and Veronica have been dating for a year now and are trying to decide if they should get engaged. That's their decision-making situation. Let's follow them through the rest of the process as a kind of case study.

Step 2. Ask God to show you the larger context and spiritual influences affecting your situation.

Sometimes we forget that God has eternal purposes he is going to accomplish. A part of those eternal purposes is his master plan for you.

Your current love-life situation is being influenced by God; he wants what's best for you. It is also being influenced by Satan, who is trying to keep you from following God and his desires for you so that you will experience the worst. So ask God to help you to look beyond the immediate circumstances to the big picture of his plan.

This is what Damien and Veronica did. Veronica, in particular, was worried that the personality differences between the two of them would doom their relationship. But as she asked God for direction, she began to see this line of thinking as being based more in fear and temptation than trust in God. She has begun to get a vision for how her traits and Damien's might be combined in a marriage that could bring glory to God.

Step 3. Entrust your concerns to God.

Who or what is the current object of your trust and faith? Each one of us would immediately like to respond, "God, of course!" But if we are honest, who are we really trusting for the results in our current circumstances? Ourselves? Our boyfriend or girl-friend? Our friends? Our family members? Available resources, whether financial, physical or something else?

God is trustworthy. He has the ability to accomplish

what concerns us (see Jeremiah 32:17). He is committed to our well-being (see Psalm 32:10). He will do what he promises (see Psalm 33:4). We can rest in his loving care and concern for us.

Damien has taken the lead in this area for his relationship with Veronica. He's a young man of bold faith, and he's helping Veronica to trust God more too. He suggested they make the following a prayer for their relationship:

> *Father God, we ask that you make this relationship every-thing you want it to be. No more and no less. Thank you for guiding us to your perfect will. Amen.*

This doesn't necessarily mean they'll wind up getting married, but it does mean they're more confident of fulfilling God's good and gracious will for them, whatever that may be.

Step 4. Prepare yourself to hear God.

Sometimes we can't discern God's direction in our lives. This might be because we have sin in our lives. It might be because we need to humble ourselves before God. It might be because we're not patient enough to wait for God. But whatever the reason, we need to remove obstacles within ourselves so that we can hear from God.

We like what Veronica and Damien are doing—spending time every week praying together. They invite God to teach them how he wants them to change. They pour out their requests for each other. It seems to us that God must love this attempt by these two young people to open themselves to him as much as possible.

Step 5. Recognize the directional signposts.

Daniel 2:28 says, "There is a God in heaven who reveals mys-teries." We know God cares about us and will show us his plan. Once we have entrusted our situation or problem into his hands, we must expect his answer.

Be alert as God reveals his will to you through …

- his Word, the Bible (2 Timothy 3:16–17)
- the Holy Spirit who indwells you (John 14:26)
- godly people (Proverbs 11:14; 15:22)
- providential circumstances (Proverbs 16:9)

Consider what recent insights, impressions, counsel or signs have made an impact on you that may be from God.

Lately, our friends Damien and Veronica have had several people they respect tell them that they seem right for each other. This is encouraging them to keep seeking God's will for a possible future life together.

Step 6. Test the step you're considering.

James 1:5 provides clear direction when it tells us, "If any of you lacks wisdom, you should ask God, who gives generously to all without finding fault, and it will be given to you."

Make sure the action you're considering is from God. Ask yourself questions like the following:

- *Does this action comply with the directions given in God's Word?*
- *Does this solution demonstrate love for God?*
- *Does this resolution demonstrate love for others?*
- *Does this direction make sense when I use reasoning that is based on God's truth?*
- *Does this revelation generate a supernatural inner peace and calmness that cannot be attributed merely to your circumstances?*

These are the kinds of questions that Veronica and Damien are wrestling with. We believe they will make the right choice in the end.

Step 7. Take the next step by faith.

Once you have worked your way through the preceding steps and believe that you know God's direction, take the next step by faith, knowing that God will redirect you if necessary. You can go forward with this assurance:

The Lord himself goes before you and will be with you; he will never leave you nor forsake you. Do not be afraid; do not be discouraged.

—Deuteronomy 31:8

Whether Damien and Veronica get engaged or not, if they used sanctified feelings and reasoning, they'll choose wisely and will be safe in the hands of God. So will you.

WHAT'S NEXT

In part 3 of this book we have looked at some practical guidelines for making yourself ready for God's best.

- Adopt godly motivates for wanting to be married. (chapter 9)
- Don't let your soul mate become your idol. (chapter 10)
- Learn from past relationship failures. (chapter 11)
- Use sanctified thinking and feeling in your relationship decisions. (chapter 12)

Think back to where you were when you started reading this book. You've learned a lot about getting ready for God's best! As we said at the beginning, when you are the right person, you'll meet the right person. If you have been applying what you have been reading, you're on your way to being the right person.

So, what is your next decision to make? What is the next step to take? Whatever it is, do it. God will be there with you.

What we're going to be getting into now is the fun stuff—how to go about finding the love of your life. You see, we want you to be ready for God's best, not just through having the right spiritual position with God, but also through conducting your search for your soul mate in the right way. This is big stuff too in its own way. Big *and* practical.

PART 4

YOUR
DATING STRATEGY

13

PURSUE "ONENESS" POTENTIAL

Knowing what God's ideal is for marriage

From God's perspective, what does an ideal marriage really look like? How does a marriage become all he intended it to be? What is God's formula for marital bliss?

God desires "oneness" in marriage. This oneness is first described in Genesis 2, and Jesus spoke of the oneness principle in the Gospel of Mark:

> "At the beginning of creation God 'made them male and female.' 'For this reason a man will leave his father and mother and be united to his wife, and the two will become one flesh.' So they are no longer two, but one."
>
> —Mark 10:6–8

This physical union is symbolic of the oneness God desires for us in marriage and applies to all the various dimensions that make us human. God wants married couples to grow into greater union with each other while simultaneously growing in intimacy with him.

As I (Brad) began to understand the various dimensions of oneness, the fog and confusion accompanying my dating relationships began to clear. I began to understand that I should not even consider marriage with someone unless I knew there was oneness potential. Furthermore, the extent of this oneness could have great potential to either hurt or enhance my intimacy with God. It only seemed reasonable that oneness potential must be a major clue in recognizing God's best match for marriage.

SPIRITUAL ONENESS

For us as Christians, our spiritual lives are guided by the directive to "love the LORD your God with all your heart and with all your soul and with all your strength" (Deuteronomy 6:5). God originally created man in such a way as to have an intimate love relationship with him. We were created to demonstrate that love by glorifying God in our worship, devotion and service. We believe that God wants this to also be the top priority in marriage as well.

Obviously, this is only possible if both people have received Jesus into their lives as their Lord and Savior. The apostle Paul warns, "Do not be yoked together with unbelievers. For what do righteousness and wickedness have in common? Or what fellowship can light have with darkness?" (2 Corinthians 6:14).

Our personal relationship and intimacy with God is the absolute highest priority to him. While Paul is clearly stating that Christians are not to marry unbelievers, this principle of being "unequally yoked" can also have implications for two believers when it comes to their theological beliefs and spiritual lives.

As I considered this, I thought about the things that affected my worship, devotion and service to God. Wouldn't it make sense that my ideal soul mate would not only share these beliefs but also appreciate that I have them? Wouldn't we both be drawn closer to God through similar worship music, types of church services and devotional activities?

In several of my dating relationships there were big differences in these areas. These women loved God and were very committed to him, but we connected with our heavenly Father in different ways. For example, one woman I dated found a liturgical, traditional worship style to be most meaningful in her spiritual walk. When I attended those services with her, I had a difficult time connecting with God. Another lady enjoyed attending a charismatic church with a very contemporary style of worship. When I went to church with her, I felt like an observer. The service didn't engage my spirit and soul—but it did engage hers! While there is nothing wrong with either of these church services, a different style of worship touches my heart and draws me closer to God.

If you are dating, try attending church together. It is a great way to learn more about each other and how God's Spirit engages with each of you. You will find that the kind of church worship and teaching you like spills over into how you spend personal time with God as well.

Imagine this scenario: Two people who have very different desires for how they worship and relate with God get married. What church will they attend together? Are they going to go to the one the husband likes? Then the wife won't feel the spiritual connection she used to by attending her former place of worship. Or maybe the husband decides they will go to the church that most benefits his wife's spiritual needs. And so he will become disconnected from his ideal form of worship. This kind of deference to the other person might seem like a very loving thing to do, but it eventually may become an obstacle to greater intimacy with God because personal worship has been compromised.

And what about devotional times together at home? How will both of you feel the same connection with God if you are not engaging with him in the same way you had before getting married?

Is your personal time with God already very special? Or do you feel the need to find a new way to energize your spiritual life? If it is the latter, then perhaps the spiritual changes your potential spouse brings into your life are exactly what God wants so you will have a more intimate relationship with him.

You may be thinking, *This seems mighty nitpicky. The import-*

ant thing isn't whose church the couple goes to, as long as they go together and focus on God.

While that is certainly far better than what happens in many relationships, is it ideal? If God placed two people on paths that lead both to greater intimacy with him and he intends for them to meet and marry at some point, wouldn't you think a sovereign God, who is intimately involved in the details of their lives, would have those paths mesh perfectly?

This was a major factor in helping me recognize Nicole as the soul mate God had selected for me. We are very much in agreement about what touches us spiritually. As a result, both of us have developed a deeper relationship with God than before we met. And we really enjoy our times of worship together and feel the gift of oneness.

Are there theological differences between you and whomever you are dating that diminish your worship and devotion to God in some way? If so, step back and ask God for more clarity in your relationship. Spiritual oneness is cultivated by worshiping and serving God in unity.

MENTAL ONENESS

The lens through which we view life determines what we see and it corresponds with choices we make. As we discussed in chapter 5, that lens is our worldview. It shapes our philosophy of life, perception of reality and decision-making values.

The apostle Paul asks, "Where is the wise person? Where is the scholar? Where is the philosopher of this age? Has not God made foolish the wisdom of the world?" (1 Corinthians 1:20). He also made the observation, "The wisdom of this world is foolishness in God's sight" (1 Corinthians 3:19).

God reveals truth and reality in the Bible. It is our guidebook for life. We have been given the Bible so that we can have a biblical point of view as we observe life. Unfortunately, many Christians live their lives based on the deceptive philosophies of this world. Although they are saved, their lives are filled with the consequences of ignorance and foolishness. Believers need to use the Bible as the ultimate authority for daily living and be committed to renewing their minds with biblical truth.

How can two people have a harmonious relationship if they are not both submitted to the authority of the Scriptures and following biblical principles? Mental oneness is cultivated by having the same foundational beliefs and philosophy of life.

EMOTIONAL ONENESS

People are emotional beings. We have deep feelings about different things. Those feelings inspire us to act. Consequently, we invest our time, money and talent into causes or activities we believe are important. We are willing to make sacrifices for causes that have engaged our heart.

We are to be motivated by our loving concern for one another. The apostle John describes it this way:

> This is how we know what love is: Jesus Christ laid down his life for us. And we ought to lay down our lives for our brothers and sisters. If anyone has material possessions and sees his brother in need but has no pity on him, how can the love of God be in that person? Dear children, let us not love with words or tongue but with actions and in truth.
>
> —1 John 3:16–18

Before I (Brad) married Nicole, I met Jamie online. She lived in a town several hours away. She was a wonderful lady who had suffered considerable abuse from her husband before their marriage ended in divorce. As we continued to talk long distance and occasionally spent time together in person, I found out that she really loved her church. Not only was it her spiritual home where she had grown tremendously in her faith, but it was also a major place of service for her. She was involved in several ministries of the church, with numerous responsibilities. It didn't take long for me to see how passionate she was about her ministry within that group of believers.

Jamie wanted me to experience her church environment, and likewise she wanted to experience mine. I soon realized, though, that Jamie was truly called to her church ministries. If we were to marry, she would have to move to my town because of commitments that made it impossible for me to leave my community. Jamie was as passionate about her ministry calling as I was about mine. And it was not possible for both to happen if we were to marry.

Was she God's perfect match for me? Only if you believe that square pegs can comfortably fit into round holes. Our sovereign God had been guiding both of our steps for many years and called us to different ministries in different places. While she had a wonderful heart for ministry, it was not directed toward mine.

What has God laid upon your heart? What do you feel passionately about? What moves you to take action? Does the person you are dating share your passions and concerns? And do you share his or hers? Emotional oneness is cultivated by being passionately involved in the same things in life.

VOLITIONAL ONENESS

While most believers acknowledge that our purpose in life is to glorify God, many do not reflect that in their daily goals and priorities. In actuality, their purpose for life may be to glorify themselves, someone else or some organization. But God created us to fulfill his purposes. The Bible explains, "We are God's handiwork, created in Christ Jesus to do good works, which God prepared in advance for us to do" (Ephesians 2:10).

God created us to do what he deems to be important, regardless of how glamorous or menial that may appear to others. We exist to serve him wholeheartedly. Is that the desire of your heart? What about the person you are dating? Is she or he living under the banner of "Not my will but God's will be done" (see Luke 22:42)?

The prophet Amos asks a rhetorical question: "Can two people walk together without agreeing on the direction?" (Amos

3:3, NLT). Are you both heading in the same direction in life? Are you in agreement about what you want to accomplish with your lives? Volitional oneness is cultivated by being committed to the same goals, priorities and purpose for life.

PHYSICAL ONENESS

God designed sexual intercourse to be a tangible symbol of the oneness he desires between a husband and wife. It's the pleasurable icing on the cake when spiritual, mental, emotional and volitional oneness exists in the relationship. And God doesn't want this dimension of the relationship to be neglected either. The apostle Paul explains,

> The husband should fulfill his marital duty to his wife, and likewise the wife to her husband. The wife does not have authority over her own body but yields it to her husband. In the same way, the husband does not have authority over his own body but yields it to his wife.
>
> —1 Corinthians 7:3–4

All too often sex is merely used to satisfy physical urges. It can be motivated by lustful passion rather than the unconditional, self-sacrificing love that God desires. It's like settling for an appetizer instead of enjoying the entire five-course meal. God wants you to have it all, but that will happen only if you do marriage his way. Physical oneness is cultivated by bonding sexually with each other in marriage.

When you are compatible in all of these critical areas, you can have a good foundation upon which you develop greater oneness in marriage. It will be much more challenging to develop the oneness that God desires for you if you don't begin your marriage with relatively the same views and priorities in each of these vital areas. Ask God to give you his wisdom as you seek to discern the oneness potential in your relationships.

14

AVOID THE "TYPE" TRAP

Getting out of the revolving-door syndrome

There you are, at some event, and a stranger of the opposite sex engages you in conversation. You talk for a while and then move on. One of your friends makes the comment "He (or she) sure seemed interested in you. Don't you want to see if you can get a date?" Your response to that question might be, "Sure do" or "No, he's (she's) not my type." These kinds of interactions usually elicit a quick, subconscious evaluation that either results in piqued interest or squelched desire for more contact.

Have you ever thought about your ideal "type"—the kind of person to whom you are consistently attracted? Your description, no doubt, is somewhat lacking because type is a blend of conscious and subconscious qualities that you personally find appealing. It's as much about feelings as it is about thought. This person just seems "right" to you; that one doesn't. Words can't adequately express the connection you sense.

PATTERNS IN YOUR RELATIONSHIPS

I (Brad) met Sherri on eHarmony back in my single days. We spent many weeks getting to know one another by phone. As we became more comfortable with each other, Sherri began to share her history of broken relationships. Frankly, I was shocked as she revealed one bad relationship after another. Eventually she asked, "Why do I always seem be attracted to guys who turn out to be jerks?" That was a good question. She realized that she had developed a pattern of getting involved with guys who would leave her feeling used and abused.

What's your history with dating relationships? Would you say the people you've dated, in general, have been compatible with you, or has your life been marked by disappointment after disappointment? If you want to have a healthy, positive, ideal soul-mate relationship, you need to have the right criteria for selecting your type of partner. The purpose of this book is to give you some guidelines that can help you recognize that person.

Back to Sherri. As our conversations became deeper, I discovered more details about Sherri and what she valued. Among other things, she was attracted to athletic, macho men. It didn't matter if they were rough around the edges. In fact, that actually added to the appeal for her. She kind of liked the bad-boy mystique. There is nothing wrong with the description I've just given, but in addition, the guys she was attracted to usually only had one thing on their mind—conquest. With each one, it wouldn't take long for Sherri to find herself going way too far and realizing she had blown it again. She didn't take the time to really think about the character qualities she wanted in a partner.

FOCUSED ON THE RIGHT CHARACTER QUALITIES

People are multifaceted beings with varying traits. You need to think about what character qualities you really want in a spouse. Does the current type of person you typically date excel in the areas you value most? If you want a soul mate who is God's best for you, the criteria you use must coincide with his. You must be willing to take some time to consider the type of person you are attracted to and make adjustments in your value system if needed.

Every person has external and internal qualities. The externals are easily seen, but the inner qualities require careful observation over time. Unfortunately, many single people place too much emphasis on the superficial externals at the expense of the deeper qualities that really make relationships work.

When God sent the prophet Samuel to anoint a new king of Israel to replace Saul, God cautioned him, "Do not consider his appearance or his height, for I have rejected him. The LORD does not look at the things man looks at. Man looks at the outward appearance, but the LORD looks at the heart" (1 Samuel 16:7).

Physical characteristics, personality and reputation relate to outward appearance. Character, purpose and spiritual maturity reflect what's in a person's heart. The correct priorities, from the most important to least valuable, should be as follows.

- Spiritual maturity: Will you be able to love and follow Jesus together?
- Purpose for life: Is what you want from life compatible with the other person's goals?
- Character qualities: Do his thoughts, words and actions demonstrate integrity?
- Reputation: Do you like what others think and say about her?
- Personality type: Do you enjoy how he interacts with you and others?
- Physical appearance: Do you like the way she looks?

It would be great if a person scored a 10 on each characteristic, but that is unlikely and unrealistic. It's vital that you give spiritual maturity, purpose and character close consideration. Spiritual maturity defines purpose and shapes character. Character establishes reputation and refines personality. Personality illuminates physical appearance. In the right sequence, these areas all get better and better.

When you think about past relationships you've had, arrange these six qualities in order of strongest to weakest for each one of those people. Do you see the same pattern repeated when you compare them? If so, this reveals the pattern of values and priorities you have used in your past decision-making. Do they reflect God's desires?

So, what happened to Sherri? The last time we spoke, she was being pulled into a relationship with a married man. Unfortunately, she was still locked in a pattern that could only end in disaster. Whenever any of us choose something different from what God wants for us, the error of our ways is eventually uncovered and we must live with the consequences of our choice.

If you have had your share of bad relationships and you don't want more disappointments, allow God to change your priorities. Otherwise, the pattern you have established will continue. If you want God's best, follow his guidance and allow him to direct you to the type of person he wants you to establish a soul mate relationship with. After all, he is the One who designed you and is most committed to your well-being..

15

THINK ABOUT "COMPATIBILITY"

Connecting on many different levels

Compatibility is a hot topic today! Google the word and you'll find results related to everything from zodiac and horoscopes (is your sign compatible with the person you are dating?), to technology (as in IBM or specific application compatibility), temperaments (take a test like Myers-Briggs) or love and romance capability indicators (there's an inventory for everything). It's enough to make your head spin—and make a confusing subject even more confusing!

Opposites attract. In chemistry, this is quite often fantastic! In relationships, that's not always so great. Initially, there's a sense of magic that comes from spending time with someone who is quite different from us. This individual is everything we are not. Together, we seem to make a whole. We appreciate the other person's differences and value what he or she brings to the relationship. But in the long term those opposite behaviors and attitudes have the potential to cause us frustration.

When it comes to relationships, compatibility is a key component. But for Christians seriously desiring a relationship that will go the distance, in what areas of the relationship is compatibility a major factor?

Does God really care if I am compatible with my mate? And how compatible is compatible enough?

There is no doubt that compatibility makes life easier. Marriage involves two people living together. When you see things similarly, it's much easier to come to decisions that both of you are happy with. But what is God's desire?

Let's take a look at what God tells us in his Word when it comes to absolutes, preferences and principles.

ABSOLUTES: GOD GIVES US A DIRECTIVE ABOUT COMPATIBILITY

As much as we want clear direction from God as to his plan for our lives, when it comes to a marriage partner there is really only one passage in the New Testament that speaks specifically to the compatibility issue. (Note that there are also verses in the New Testament that deal with eligibility for marriage, such as in the case of divorce and remarriage in Matthew 5, but right now we are discussing compatibility.) And that directive is very important.

> Do not be yoked together with unbelievers.
> —2 Corinthians 6:14

This is a reiteration of a principle God gave the Israelites in the Old Testament, directing them not to marry anyone outside of the Jewish nation. Why? Because marriage has a significant influence on who we become. God knows that to be in a life union with someone who has the same foundation (Christ) as we do will be best for us.

That isn't a lot of direction, but it is very clear. God wants us to be in a relationship with someone who believes in him. The only directive he has for us, the only absolute he has given us in Scripture, is that the person we marry be a believer. We know many single people who are willing to compromise when it comes to this directive from God.

What does it mean to be in a relationship with a believer? First of all, a believer is someone who has a personal relationship with God because he or she believes that Jesus Christ died on the cross to pay the price for sin. That is the very foundation on which to start. After you have established common ground as a believer, compatibility on how you are actually living out your faith can really be a factor.

Early in the relationship, or even before you begin dating someone, discuss the degree of his or her commitment to Christ. Be thinking about how to ask questions such as "How did you come to know Jesus personally?" "What is helping you to grow in your relationship with God?" "How important is it to you to fellowship with other believers?" "Do you desire to be involved in groups within the church?" "How do you worship God?" Then consider: do you like what you're discovering about the person you are dating?

What about the person's level of involvement in church? Does he or she attend worship services regularly? Is this person involved in a ministry? Are you coming from a more traditional or contemporary background? If so, can you accept someone from a different background?

Why do you need to discuss these areas? Because God's top priority is that each one of us has a growing love relationship with him. This priority supersedes all other relationships and needs to influence all the other areas of our life. This one factor will ultimately have the greatest impact on your marriage and in experiencing God's best with your spouse.

God's absolute is that we marry a believer, but there are other priorities that will help guide us toward compatibility.

PRIORITIES: GOD GIVES US GUIDANCE FOR WISE DECISION-MAKING

In the Bible, the prophet Amos asks this important question: "Can two people walk together without agreeing on the direction?" (Amos 3:3, NLT). God has blessed you with a good mind to ascertain the stability of your relationship. Strong relationships are built on good thinking (not just exciting feelings)! We believe that God's Holy Spirit gives us wisdom—and we can use that wisdom in every area of our lives, including our relationships.

Take time to think about this: Do you and your potential mate agree on the direction you are heading? Not just with the relationship, but in the other areas of your life as well? There are seven major topics that are important to consider as you answer this question: spiritual maturity, purpose for life, expectations, character, intelligence, attachments and life experiences. Set aside some time to think about each of these areas and then have a serious discussion with your partner.

Spiritual Maturity

In previous chapters, we have already emphasized how important a role God plays in the health of a marriage. Where do you both stand with regard to your relationship with the Lord? Are your hearts devoted and yielded to him? Is there an observable consistency in your spiritual lives?

Do you enjoy similar worship styles and agree on basic Bible truths? Marriage is intended to be a three-way relationship, with God being the ultimate authority and harmonizer. If he isn't at the center of your relationship, you are dooming your marriage to mediocrity at best.

Purpose for Life

What are you living for—short term and long term? What drives you? Family? Fun? Ministry? Career? Money? Success? Possessions (house, car, clothes, grown-up toys such as a boat or technology gadgets)? Hobbies? Prestige? Recognition?

Are you and your potential spouse on the same page with regard to your purpose in life? Purpose is a target for your life. It is what drives your decisions about the use of your time, abilities and financial resources. If you and your spouse are aiming at different targets, it will result in disagreements and relational tension. Beyond that, if you are choosing targets that God doesn't want, then from an eternal perspective, you are essentially wasting your life.

Expectations

In the excitement of a new relationship, people often fail to discuss life expectations. It's just fun to be together. However, at some point, it's important to have a discussion about personal expectations. If this relationship leads to marriage, what are your expectations within the relationship? Are you both going to work? What about children? Yes or no? How many? Who will be responsible for their care? How about finances? Separate or joint? Who will be responsible for what? What are the expensive items you are hoping to have once you are married? How do you want to spend your time, and what expectations do you have for your mate in this regard? What are your views on sex? What are your thoughts on opposite-sex friendships and associations once you are married? What standard of living is your goal and how are you going to get there?

Many people assume answers to these questions based on how they grew up and what their parents modeled. Because the answers to these questions seem obvious or normal, they may not even discuss the issues until conflict arises once they are married. Some of these issues can be difficult or awkward to talk about, but they are critical to a compatible relationship down the road.

Character

Does it matter to you what kind of character qualities your mate has? A person's character affects and essentially becomes his or her reputation. Is that important to you?

All too often people overlook character flaws in dating relationships because they have become emotionally involved and are "in love." They think that they can deal with troubling attitudes and behavior later. But character is usually shaped over a long period of time by a person's life experiences. It is foolhardy to expect changes after marriage. Sometimes dramatic transformation can occur within a person through a major life-altering event or crisis, but don't count on that. The character qualities you see while dating are typically what you will be living with after marriage.

Intelligence

When it comes to relationships, we believe intellectual compatibility isn't about what schools we've attended or what degrees were obtained. It's about the way intelligence affects our communication. Effective communication is vital to the health of any marriage. The *level* of education that both mates have is certainly an initial indicator, but it is not all inclusive. What is important here, is *how* we go about communicating, and that can be influenced by our intelligence. Our overall intellectual capabilities and experiences have an impact on the way we interact with people. One person may be a concrete thinker, while the other is comfortable with abstract concepts. Or someone may have a love for knowledge but no practical wisdom in relating it to life. Or when it comes to problem solving, one person may be very logical while the other person thinks more outside of the box and creatively. The bottom line is whether you are both on the same wavelength when you talking with each other. Is communication enjoyable or a chore? Are you communicating on the same intellectual level?

Attachments

Every person lives within a cluster of commitments that have accumulated over time. Some represent responsibilities or promises made to friends or family. Other commitments reflect the deep-seated desires of the individual. These attachments greatly affect what a person brings into a relationship and what will influence future decisions.

For example, take a look at your potential mate's friend base. With whom does he or she keep company? Are these good, honest, caring people? Are they believers?

What else is your potential mate committed to? Children from a previous marriage? Elderly parents requiring care? Pets? Vocational commitments? Educational goals? Living in a particular geographic location?

Are you willing to accept those attachments? Some represent commitments that should never be broken. Others represent strong personal preferences that can be set aside, if necessary, for the sake of the relationship. But even those can crop up later because they are so ingrained in the makeup of the person.

Consider, too, your own attachments. What are your deep-seated desires?

When you marry, attachments should be accepted as part of the union. It is shortsighted to overlook this reality.

Life Experiences

What kinds of life experiences are both of you bringing to the relationship? How have those experiences shaped you? Be honest with yourself and your mate. Share great experiences as well as painful or hurtful ones. What you have experienced in life greatly contributed to the formation of your character. Cultural influences, family upbringing, difficulties and successes all have profoundly shaped who you are as a person.

While it is certainly possible for two very different people to have a wonderful, fulfilling marriage, it is also a fact that when two people can relate to each other's life experiences, marriage is more satisfying.

PREFERENCE: GOD GIVES US FREEDOM TO SATISFY OUR PERSONAL TASTE

God has made each one of us a unique individual. And within that individuality comes personal preferences and tastes. Although the Bible makes it clear that we should only build a marriage with someone who is a Christian, there is still a lot of room for us to make a personal choice. When it comes to personality, appearance and interests, we have a lot of options!

For example, in the area of personality, do you prefer someone outgoing, reserved, brainy, fun-loving, compassionate, compliant, sweet, tough, steady ...? How about in the area of appearance? What are you looking for by way of age, height, body type? Is someone's personal style important to you? What about personal hygiene? What is most attractive to you and your tastes?

A person's interests are usually important when it comes

to personal preference. What do you like to do? Are you more of a homebody, or do you want to go out several times a week? Are you more into leisure activities, outdoor activities, thrill-seeking opportunities, the arts? What are your political views? Can you be with someone who doesn't share those exact opinions? How about health? How focused are you on physical fitness?

How important is it to you—and to your mate—that you share similar views and interests? How much are you willing to agree to disagree? Are you open to new ideas and experiences?

IN A NUTSHELL

How much does God really care about compatibility? God cares a great deal about our faith compatibility! The bottom line is that it is important to build a relationship with a person who is a Christian. But beyond that, it may be God's will for two people who are quite different to be married, as long as they are a committed to him and to each other.

But don't forget, God's primary purpose in marriage is not our happiness—that is a bonus. His main objective is to accomplish his plan for us. Remember Hosea? God wanted him to marry a harlot and remain faithful to her. That marriage became an illustration of Israel's unfaithfulness to God while he remained faithful to Israel. (See the book of Hosea in the Old Testament.)

It can be difficult to remain committed in a marriage that is less than ideal, especially if one of the spouses is not a believer. But the Bible instructs us,

> If a Christian woman has a husband who is not a believer and he is willing to continue living with her, she must not leave him. For the Christian wife brings holiness to her marriage, and the Christian husband brings holiness to his marriage.
> —1 Corinthians 7:13–14, NLT

God wants to use you as his instrument for blessing and

transformation even in a difficult marriage. However, if you are single and in the process of finding a mate, consider these compatibility guidelines seriously. Don't intentionally put yourself into an ill-advised marriage.

You are making a choice about who to marry! Compatibility is important but not an absolute requirement in every area. However, we need to use wisdom and good judgment whenever we are considering marriage. In the book of James we are told, "If any of you lacks wisdom, you should ask God, who gives generously to all without finding fault, and it will be given to you" (1:5). Ask God for the wisdom you need and depend on his guidance.

If you are currently in a serious relationship, do you believe that this person could be God's best for you? If you have questions or concerns or an uneasiness about the relationship, give yourself more time to gain perspective on the relationship. Think more, talk more with your prospective mate and ask trusted friends for their thoughts and opinions about the relationship.

Hold on to the fact that God wants his best for you in everything you do, including choosing a mate. Obey his absolute, pursue his wisdom and trust his will for your life.

16

LOOK FOR "CHEMISTRY"

Enhancing or imploding your relationship

Chemistry … it's talked about a lot … on the college campus, in the workplace, and among acquaintances, family and friends. We're not referring here to the science of chemistry, which controls and measures different substances, but to romantic chemistry—which is rarely controlled or measured! Have you experienced it? That *zing* in a dating relationship that you can't quite explain but that is very real?

Whereas compatibility is more cognitive and head based, chemistry is emotive—anchored in feelings. And oh, are those feelings nice!

Sometimes people confuse compatibility and chemistry and think they are the same. But they're not. As we discussed in the preceding chapter, compatibility is about common values, similar beliefs and shared priorities. However, chemistry is an emotional connection that is possible between people who may be quite different.

TYPES OF RELATIONAL CHEMISTRY

There are actually several types of relational chemistry. (Yes, chemistry can be experienced in more than just romantic relationships.)

One type of relational chemistry that you may have experienced is *purpose chemistry*. Do you remember a time when you found yourself really enjoying a project because of a great connection with a teammate? Not only did you work well together, but you also had a common bond—wanting to see the cause or team succeed. You have great synergy with people like this because you are working together toward a mutual goal. This connection is based on a shared commitment and dedication to the accomplishment of something you all feel passionately about.

With purpose chemistry, we bring out the best in each other, whether we're leading, following or working side by side. The Bible gives us an illustration of this type of chemistry in the relationship of Joshua and Caleb. (You can read all about it in Numbers 13 and 14, Deuteronomy 1, Joshua 14 and Judges 1.)

Another type of relational chemistry is *friendship chemistry*. Do you have a good friend you enjoy and get along with especially well? Someone who's your kindred spirit? Someone you can be yourself with because he or she instinctively understands you? You're comfortable kidding around or joking with this friend because you know you can be completely transparent with this special person. You're comfortable and secure in this relationship. You feel that when you are with this person, you are in a no-judgment zone. The relationship brings you joy, comfort and security.

This type of chemistry doesn't give you a *zing*, but it does provide you with a secure bond of honesty and loyalty that can only be found in a true friend. The Bible illustrates this kind of chemistry in the relationships of David and Jonathan as well as Ruth and Naomi.

Now back to romantic chemistry and the *zing*. Romantic chemistry is usually triggered by external characteristics such as personality, appearance, interests and reputation. On a subconscious level, you have created a composite of external traits that make up the type of person you desire. And when you meet someone like that, you sense a magnetic attraction that can become irresistible.

Romantic chemistry is often exciting and sexually charged. You may find yourself obsessively focused on the person who has become the object of your love and affection. That person is the star of your daydreams. You look for every opportunity to be together. You want more of the other person on every level. This type of chemistry (within the boundaries of marriage) is talked about in full-blown intensity in the Bible's Song of Songs.

CHEMISTRY THAT WORKS FOR YOU INSTEAD OF AGAINST YOU

What chemistry should you be looking for with your soul mate? Ideally all three. Unfortunately, too many couples settle for romantic chemistry and try building their marriage on that alone. Over time, they discover that this is a rather shallow foundation for a lifelong commitment.

Essentially, all three types of chemistry are involved with how you get along especially well with someone, albeit in different ways. You just naturally understand each other. You have a genuine appreciation and understanding for who the other person is and what drives him or her. You want to be together.

I (Brad) remember the first time Nicole and I met. We had lunch and then spent the afternoon together just wandering through the mall getting to know each other better. That first day we met, I was attracted to Nicole. *Zing!* We had already communicated quite a bit by e-mail and phone, so I knew we were exceptionally compatible. Good thing, because when you feel the *zing*, your head can easily take a backseat to your heart. *Zing* usually overrules the logic of compatibility. And while that may be fun in the short run, it can really cause problems later.

For the next several months, Nicole and I had a lot of fun dates, enjoying the summer and doing the touristy things you otherwise never seem to get around to doing. And while all of that is fun, it is also somewhat artificial because that isn't what everyday life is like.

I decided we should take on some project together to see how much purpose chemistry we had. Nicole had family coming from out of state to visit for a week, and so we decided to tackle a remodeling project in her home. That was a different way to spend time together! Nothing like seeing what your soul mate can do with a sledgehammer.

That project enabled us to experience other aspects of each other. We discovered that we work well together and greatly enjoy doing a variety of projects as a team. In fact, now that we've been married for several years, we are even writing this book together!

Over time, we have also developed exceptional friendship chemistry. We are kindred spirits. We are able to be totally transparent around each other and not fear rejection or disapproval. We feel so blessed to have all three kinds of chemistry in our relationship. Every day, we rejoice in the love relationship God has made possible for us.

In God's creative genius, he has given us the capacity to deeply connect with other people in these same ways, and we can bring him glory by honoring him and his intentions in all our relationships. However, without God's guidance, the feeling of chemistry can lead to inappropriate thoughts and behavior. We need to be on guard against letting our feelings overpower our reliance on God to guide us.

Purpose chemistry and friendship chemistry have pretty definite boundaries, but when it comes to romantic chemistry, all kinds of confusion can arise. Romantic chemistry can be especially powerful, and it can enhance relationships when appropriate, but it can also be perplexing. This is because of the exciting physical component that plays into romantic chemistry.

Today's culture seems to overemphasize the physical chemistry between two people, often at the expense of developing a solid relationship. Because of all the messages being sent through the media, people can become obsessed with the desire for romantic chemistry. We can ignore warning signs in the relationship because the *zing* makes us feel so special. It's wise to ask yourself, *Are we coming together and helping each other build a solid relationship, or is this just a sexual spark?*

Once the powerful physical component of romantic chemistry comes into your relationship, it can be difficult to think logically or to focus on other aspects of growing together.

Building a relationship on romantic chemistry alone can often lead to an explosion!

Sometimes romantic chemistry is not immediate but develops over time in a relationship that starts out with a different focus. This can often be ideal, because we have already gotten to know the other person without our romantic feelings distorting the view.

Regardless of how a relationship develops, God wants to be the foundation of it. Don't let romantic chemistry cloud your vision or cause you to take your eyes off God. While romantic chemistry can be exciting, God's leading and instruction will ultimately make a relationship succeed.

> The prudent understand where they are going,
> but fools deceive themselves.
>
> —Proverbs 14:8, NLT

17

Don't Rush "Commitment"

Looking before you leap

How strong is your relationship? The strength and longevity of a relationship are determined by the degree of commitment both people have to being together.

Commitment usually begins with attraction and desire. As we get to know the other person better, our desire for the relationship will either grow or diminish. The big question is, what is your objective for the relationship? The answer to that question will determine how well you want to get to know the other person and how aggressively you seek to move the relationship to another level of commitment.

It is wise to recognize that there are stages of commitment within any relationship. It's not all or nothing. Commitment grows by degrees with time.

THE PROCESS OF COMMITMENT

There is a cyclical process by which you can move from one commitment level to the next. This process may seem a bit clinical, but understanding the process will help you to see your relationship as an adventure rather than being caught up in a whirlwind. One process uses planning to make it successful; the other progression just happens, usually without precautions, and all too often ends with some devastation.

> Attraction >> Discovery >> Evaluation >> Commitment >> Cultivation >

First, the cycle begins with *attraction*. You notice the other person and for some reason you desire to get to know him or her better. You want to find out more about the other by communicating with this person or perhaps by asking others about him or her. This is part of the *discovery* step. What you learn through discovery should lead you to *evaluation*. Here, based on what you now know, you decide whether or not it is wise to become more involved with this person. If the answer is yes, you make a *commitment* to go to another level. And then you seek ways to *cultivate* the relationship, thereby developing increased attraction and desire. From there, the process starts over, taking you to new, deeper levels of commitment.

Each new level of commitment should be based on favorable insights you have gained through greater understanding of the person. Regrettably, we can get ahead of ourselves by jumping steps when we are too eager to become romantically involved or anxious to get married.

Believe me, I (Brad) know. By the time I met Nicole for our first date, I was already convinced that she was my long-awaited soul mate because of the list of specific criteria God had given me during preceding years. She perfectly fit what I believed was an impossible standard. Although I had the benefit of such revelation, she did not. We obviously had a dilemma. I could repeatedly try to persuade her to be my wife, or I could back off and wait for God to move her through the various levels of commitment. I chose to let God cultivate her heart for me. For the next several months, I concentrated on finding fun things we could do together and gave Nicole the time she needed to discern what God was telling her about me. And it worked! Otherwise, we wouldn't be writing this book together.

5 LEVELS OF COMMITMENT

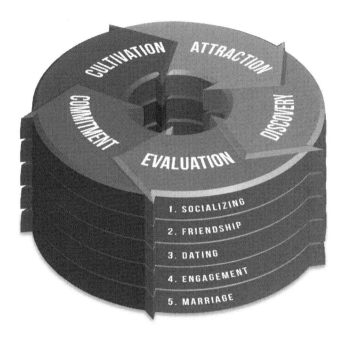

Level 1. Socializing

Level 1 represents the first stage of getting to know someone. You meet someone at a group activity, or while out with friends, or perhaps through online dating. You feel safe because you are with other people or can remain anonymous while communicating online. During this stage of the relationship, it is important to find out what you can to determine whether you can trust this person enough to let him or her know who you are and where you live.

Level 2. Friendship

Assuming you have found out enough about the other person to determine trustworthiness, you are now willing to spend time together alone or as part of a group. This is where you develop a friendship and explore compatibility. It is also a time to keep reins on your heart. It is easy to bypass this stage and jump right into a romantic relationship with someone if there is a strong attraction. But wait! If you move too quickly, your head will not have the opportunity to discover how compatible you are. And you don't want to pass this stage too soon, because after this your objectivity can easily be victimized by your passion.

Level 3. **Dating / Courtship**

When you sense God confirming that you have common values, similar beliefs and shared priorities, you can now be more free to follow your heart into the joy of romance. Yes, you may be in love and it has you walking on clouds. You've decided that this person could very well become your future mate. It is a time for both of you to demonstrate trustworthiness, sacrificial love and devotion to keeping God the center of your relationship. Because your eyes are glazing over, be careful to listen to the impressions your godly friends and family members have about the two of you. At this stage, their objectivity will be better than yours. Are they confirming what you think God has been showing you? If not, slow down and re-evaluate.

Level 4. **Engagement**

Based on everything God has revealed to you, you're convinced that this is the soul mate he has planned for you. At the right moment, the question is asked and the proposal is accepted. Wow! You are engaged to a wonderful person! And soon you will be married.

But you are not married yet. This can be a time of great temptation. You are emotionally connected with this person and it is easy to become more physically involved than God wants. Remember, you want God's blessing on your marriage. That means you are still committed to following his principles instead of worldly patterns.

From a worldly perspective, it might make sense to move in together and "try things out" before you make the marriage commitment. After all, how can you be totally sure you will really enjoy married life without experimenting first? But it is a matter of trust. Do you believe God has good reasons for not wanting you to engage in premarital sex? He designed you and invented sex. Do you really want to bet your future happiness on what someone else is telling you rather than what your Creator God has decreed as the pathway to the best?

One more caution during the engagement stage: more time and different circumstances will provide additional insights about each other. Some people come into engagement convinced that this marriage is God's will, only to have some dramatic event shatter their incomplete perception of their intended. Now what? Doubts exist but plans have already been made. Many a couple have continued into marriage because they felt trapped by circumstances. It is never too late to say no if that is the right thing to do. Use your engagement time to confirm your decision.

Level 5. **Marriage**

The big day comes and you stand before your family and friends to exchange wedding vows. You promise yourself to your mate for better or worse in an exclusive, sacrificial, intimate relationship, for the rest of your life. As momentous as this event is, you may be surprised to discover you don't feel any different afterward. Surely, if this is God's best choice for you, it should be accompanied with emotional fanfare, shouldn't it? But what you don't feel doesn't alter the fact that now, before God, the two of you are one. And that is what God desires in your marriage. Review chapter 13 and make the pursuit of oneness a priority as you begin this new journey together with God.

MOVING FORWARD CAREFULLY

Here are a few cautions you should keep in mind as you proceed in any relationship.

Do you know enough about the other person to make a greater commitment to the relationship?

Do you both have the same objective in mind? Sometimes one person only wants friendship, while the other desires romance. Or maybe one person wants to be romantically involved but has no desire for marriage. Yet romantic involvement without the potential of marriage is foolish. It will only lead to heartbreak and disappointment.

If you both have the same objective in mind, but the other person is not willing to move as quickly as you, give him or her the time needed for discovery and evaluation so the other will be comfortable when making a deeper commitment.

If you are at different commitment levels, don't fool yourself into believing that the relationship is stronger than it really is, just because of your higher degree of commitment. The strength of your relationship is actually determined by the lowest present level of commitment.

Premature commitment occurs by rushing the process and skipping steps. It will result in backpedaling and frustration. Allow the relationship to develop naturally according to God's timetable.

18

WHERE TO "CIRCULATE"

Walking where God leads

How will you meet the soul mate God has for you? We're sure you have been looking for the answer to that question with every turning page in this book. While only God knows the precise answer, we can certainly share what we discovered on our journey. Hopefully the Holy Spirit will use what we share in this chapter to give you some inspiration.

It has been said, "It is difficult to steer a car that isn't moving." Unless God is planning to make an ideal-mate delivery to your front door, you need to be willing to go where believers gather. We want to give you some ideas about how to take some faith steps that God can use to guide you.

COMMUNITY OPPORTUNITIES

Notice we said "where believers gather." In our society, bars are a typical place singles go to meet other singles. We hope you are not tempted to explore that venue. Would a person with the traits you want in your soul mate be hanging out there? If you are looking for God's best, remember the important qualities we considered in previous chapters.

So, where can you more easily expect to find believers with the right kind of values in your community? An obvious place to start is church. Depending on the size of your church family, you may already know the singles who attend and have concluded that God's match isn't there.

Next, you should consider other similar churches where you would feel comfortable attending events and meeting fellow believers. However, it is very important that you not go on a hunt. You are not on a mate-shopping trip. You are just participating and fellowshipping within the larger body of Christ—encouraging, serving and sharing the gifts God has given you for the benefit of others. If God has the right person there for you, he will make the introductions. You are not going looking. You are going to participate in the way God would want. It is his responsibility to orchestrate meetings and conversations.

Do you understand the difference? By faith you go, serve and participate in God's family as he leads. And as you do, God will guide you into relationships he has for you. Often those relationships are what God is using to get you and others ready for what he has planned around the next bend on the road of your soul-mate journey with him. Be sensitive to the Spirit leading you to other community groups or events where you can be his ambassador while meeting people.

Before we move on from this section, we want to caution you to be careful who you trust, even in church settings. Sometimes there are wolves in sheep's clothing attending church functions primarily so they can prey on the unsuspecting. We have heard stories from women who were deceived by such men at church singles events. They thought they had met Mr. Right, only to find out Mr. Wolf was interested in nothing more than sex.

We can easily be fooled when we are least expecting deception. Timothy warns us, "Evil people and impostors will flourish. They will deceive others and will themselves be deceived" (2 Timothy 3:13, NLT). Stay alert. Ask the Holy Spirit to reveal the truth about what is going on. Do not let your emotions blind you to reality. Be familiar with the process of commitment in chapter 17 and don't move from one commitment level to the next too soon.

Where else can you find believers? Bring Christ into your conversations at work, the gym, even while waiting in line at the supermarket. This will not only strengthen your commitment to bring God into your daily life, but it can also open up new friendships with otherwise unknown believers.

Rob did just that. While waiting to buy his groceries, he noticed a woman in the line in front of him without a wedding ring on. She seemed slightly impatient with waiting in line, so he used it as an opportunity to strike up a conversation. She was trying to decide whether she could actually get through this line and make it to work on time. Rob used this moment to share his faith that God could take care of even that problem. The comment about faith became the start of a new friendship that later developed into a dating relationship.

While you are living life, you meet people and can watch for opportunities to meet their needs. You might strike up a conversation while taking the bus. Or at the local dog park, if animals are your thing. Meet people by going to concerts, museums or the library. All of these are places where chance meetings can happen, and they are also places you can find something to enjoy. You are on a journey with God, so don't forget to notice the adventure.

ONLINE DATING

Technology has sure brought us a long way from the days of advertising for a mail-order bride. Online matchmaking and dating websites are now the rage.

I (Brad) had no interest in being on dating websites. However, a friend convinced me to try eHarmony. I reluctantly completed my profile and entered the arena of cyber-matchmaking. I was astonished by how quickly I received notifications about women who supposedly would be a good fit for me. Over time, this resulted in several long-distance friendships. Even though I was impressed by eHarmony's test for twenty-nine dimensions of compatibility, I quickly discovered that it could not accomplish what God can do as a Matchmaker. Nevertheless, it was a good place for me to meet people and develop relationships.

I (Nicole) was drawn to Internet matchmaking, not for myself, but as a tool to help a coworker re-enter the dating scene.

She had been alone for eight years and had a heart that longed to love and be loved. I told her about a friend of mine who had tried Internet dating. I thought the two of us should test the waters and see what was out there.

I went through the enrollment process on the Christian Mingle website first so that I could have some experience before we worked on getting her enrolled. Posting pictures wasn't a priority for me, and I received a few messages suggesting I shouldn't be on the site without completing my profile. Since I was doing this to help a friend, I didn't take the message personally and I trudged on through the gauntlet of steps for first-timers.

During the process, I was matched with a man who lived several hours away. As we communicated by email, he recommended a website he had created that offered Christians practical dating advice. I thought he lived too far away and was too old for me, so I didn't consider him as husband material.

His *Soul Mates by God* website, however, piqued my interest and caused me to have further contact with him. The thought that God could have a perfect partner for me was inspiring. And little did I know that perfect partner would be with the man who lived too far away and was older than I would have chosen!

I was amazed that, despite the fact I was on this dating site to help a friend (who, I might add, got cold feet and never joined), God used it to connect me with my future husband. I am still in awe of how Brad and I continue to find things out about each other that give us a special sense of unity and oneness.

What about you? Would you like to try matchmaking websites to meet people online?

My (Brad's) view about these online dating sites changed significantly once I started using them. I participated on several dating sites during the four years prior to meeting Nicole. I found several advantages to online dating sites I had not realized before.

When you meet someone in person and want to pursue a relationship, it is usually because you have experienced some romantic chemistry. While this is exciting, the *zing* we discussed in chapter 16 can cloud your judgment in finding out more about that person before you become too involved. Online, you start by discovering several things about someone from his or her profile before you ever begin communicating with the person. Then, when you exchange messages through the site, it is much easier to ask bold, direct questions about things that are important to you. Questions that will quickly reveal character qualities and commitment to Christ.

Since my life didn't leave me with much time to devote to developing the online experience, I cut through some of the normal get-acquainted niceties and quickly jumped to some of the character issues that were important to me. It may come as a shock, but a question I would ask early on—without letting the other person know my view—was whether she was open to premarital sex. I saw this as a way to quickly gain some indication of how committed a woman was to God's standards. What a bombshell!

If a woman on the website were desperate for a relationship, she would generally hedge her answer so as not to discourage a guy who was probably wanting premarital sex. In that case, I knew right away where she stood in her obedience to God on that issue. And for me, that was an immediate "not interested." On the other hand, if a woman responded "No way!" to my question without hesitation, I knew she had the kind of spiritual commitment and values I was seeking in a marriage partner. This was one of my important discovery questions. You could use this question yourself or come up with others that apply to what's important to you.

At any rate, I can't imagine myself ever asking that kind of question in person. With online dating, I was able to find out key things in a short amount of time that I may not have even discovered after six or more months of in-person dating.

The online dating process also makes it much easier to carefully move through the first level or two of the process of commitment explained in chapter 17 before trusting someone with too much personal information about yourself.

If done right, some sites can be a great tool for meeting others. I only want to mention two—eHarmony and Christian Mingle. I am sure there are many good sites available, but I also know of others that I believe are not very helpful places for Christians to meet other Christians.

CAUTIONS TO CONSIDER

Here are some more considerations for you as you contemplate online dating:

Profile Privacy

Privacy is something you need to consider before signing up with a dating site. Do you care who sees your picture and profile with online matchmaking? If this is a concern, the eHarmony system does it best. On eHarmony, you receive matches based on profile analyses. If there is a high degree of compatibility between members, eHarmony makes both parties aware of the match. While Christian Mingle and others alert you to matches based on their methodology, they also make it possible to run independent searches of member profiles. Based on the search criteria, anyone can find your profile regardless of compatibility factors unless your profile setting is turned to "private."

Matching Methods

The eHarmony test for twenty-nine dimensions of compatibility is the most extensive computer matching methodology. Christian Mingle uses their COMPASS test to evaluate more than one hundred personality factors plus *The Color Code* personality test. Some of the other dating sites use matching methods that are based more on the external characteristics that normally attract people to each other without as serious a consideration of the internal qualities that we see as vital to a successful marriage. (See chapter 15 as well as the Soul Mate Compatibility Guide in the appendix.)

Type of Members

Some dating websites are more diverse in the kinds of people they attract than others. Some websites are more focused on dating and casual relationships than on serious relationships leading to marriage. Both eHarmony and Christian Mingle have many marriage-minded members. Because Christian Mingle caters to individuals who want a relationship based on a religious foundation, their member profiles use questions that draw out Christian values and beliefs.

Online Daters Beware

I (Nicole) had the positive experience of meeting my husband on an Internet dating site, but it can also be a place for those who wish to prey on the unsuspecting. Why is it that, when it comes to love and companionship, we can become so desperate as to not notice the warning signs of an insincere relationship?

Julie, one of my friends, decided that she would try online dating. She was receiving the most heart-warming emails. With regret, she realized she wasn't the only woman receiving these emails. After some time, it became apparent that she was getting a recycled email. Her name was simply replacing the last email recipient's name.

The emails were written in a way that would appeal to almost any woman. After being captivated by the message, the women would volunteer information necessary to take the relationship to a deeper level. That new level of involvement would inevitably involve a plea for a quick loan because the man had a temporary cash flow problem brought on by unexpected car expenses, a family emergency, or some other crisis. This money scammer was targeting women who he thought were most susceptible. I later discovered that the same kind of scams were happening on other dating sites as well.

Julie contacted the website company, and that man was banned from using their system again. Julie then decided to try a different site, where God led her to her soul mate. And yet there are other women who give up on Internet dating because of these scams.

God uses many different ways in helping us to mature in our faith and trust in him. Internet dating sites can be a tool for just that purpose

CIRCULATE, BUT DON'T HUNT!

Relationships are developed through contact, not isolation. Does God want you to participate in more church or community events? Does he want you to meet believers online? Where does he want you to connect with more of his family? Ask God to lead you where he wants you to spend time with his other children. He will guide you.

It's important to remember that when you participate in events or meet people online, you shouldn't go to get but rather to give. I know you want to find your soul mate. It's natural to be looking around at people to see if any of them could be a prospective mate. But that's window shopping, and it's easy to begin to think of the places you go as soul-mate department stores where you might find the kind of partner you want. That isn't the attitude or focus God intends for you.

When you are hunting, you are trusting in your abilities to find what you are seeking, rather than trusting God to show you what he wants you to see. Reach out and get to know people for who they are, not for what you might get from them. "So encourage each other and build each other up, just as you are already doing" (1 Thessalonians 5:11, NLT).

Be an encourager and servant. Look for opportunities to demonstrate love and acceptance. Minister to the needs of others with right motives. And while you are humbly engaged in helping and building up your brothers and sisters in Christ, God will be leading you where he wants you to go. He will be introducing you to the people he wants you to meet. He will be orchestrating the circumstances through which you will finally connect with that special person he has for you. Who knows? Perhaps it's even someone you have known for a long time but you need to have your blinders removed.

> The LORD directs the steps of the godly. He
> delights in every detail of their lives.
>   —Psalm 37:23, NLT

Circulate, but don't hunt. Follow God and expect him to lead you where he wants you to go.

CONCLUSION

Are you unsure what to do next? Are you unwilling to move forward until you can be certain of the outcome? I (Brad) understand. It took many years after my divorce for me to be willing toconsider marriage again. I was in shell shock over what had happened to my first marriage. How could I ever entrust my heart to a woman again? How could I be absolutely sure a second marriage would last?

It took a long time for me to accept that there aren't any guarantees about "living happily ever after." Marriage is a faith journey. It requires faith that God will lead you to the right person. And it requires faith that you and your spouse will continue to follow the marriage path God desires for you both. That's why a dynamic day-by-day relationship with God is so important for both spouses, if their marriage is to thrive. It is only as we remain faithful to God that our marriage will become all he wants it to be.

TAKE ONE STEP OF FAITH

Are you ready to move forward with God by taking some faith steps? Over the years, I have learned that trying to plan my own course is futile. I want to figure everything out. I want to have contingency plans for anything that might go wrong. But there are far too many unknowns. We cannot predict all the changes affecting our future. Fortunately, we don't have to. God knows and sees the future clearly. We just need to trust him and follow where he leads.

So, what does it really mean to follow where God is leading? I usually notice God's guidance in various ways after they have happened. But there have been two occasions in my life when God chose to dramatically demonstrate how effectively and precisely he can guide me. I won't go into the specifics of the circumstances, but I will say that in both cases, unknown to me, God planted thoughts in my mind, literally directed my steps, prompted me to look where he wanted, influenced what I said and caused me to see what he wanted me to see. In both situations, I was astounded by what he helped me to find. No amount of human effort could have accomplished what he chose to do for me within the span of a few hours. Without knowing it, I had been completely controlled by the Holy Spirit. God literally took me where he wanted so I would gain a glimpse of his supernatural intervention in my life.

God is more capable and involved in guiding your steps and orchestrating your circumstances than you can imagine. King Solomon wrote, "A person's steps are directed by the LORD. How then can anyone understand their own way?" (Proverbs 20:24).

Solomon continued to explain, "We can make our plans, but the LORD determines our steps" (Proverbs 16:9, NLT). Think about that. Sometimes we create elaborate plans that we believe will take us where we want to go, but we developed those plans with limited knowledge and foresight. God has no limitations.

What if instead of focusing our attention on some intended goal or destination in the future, we only concentrated on discerning the next step God has for us? Then we take that step by faith. After that, we again seek his guidance for another step. Do you realize that if you continue to apply this next-step principle, you will eventually arrive at the destination God desires for you?

What if you applied this principle to your soul-mate journey, *with* God? He *wants* to take you by the hand and walk with you, but you need to cooperate with him.

Picture a father walking down a dimly lit, winding pathway holding the hand of his child. The child doesn't know how difficult the path may become, but the father does. He has traveled it before. The child doesn't know what scary things may be lurking in the shadows, but the father does. He has encountered them all before. The child doesn't know how much farther until they reach their destination, but the father does. He has been there before.

But what happens if the child lets go of his father's hand and takes off on his own? He will experience fear, confusion, worry and frustration.

The child can enjoy the adventure as long as his father is beside him. The child can feel safe as the father leads. The child trusts his father. The child knows that the father is watching out for him. This is what cooperating with God looks like.

TRUST GOD FOR YOUR SOUL MATE

God wants us to rely on him and to realize that he is the source of all the blessings that come into our lives. Every good and perfect gift is from above, coming down from the Father of the heavenly lights, who does not change like shifting shadows.

—James 1:17

God wants the best for you, and he wants you to trust him for it. He has it all figured out. He has a glorious future planned for you. But it requires that you turn over the control of your life to him. He wants you to trust him with everything. He wants you to have complete faith in him so you can be at peace with your circumstances. He desires for you to rest and not be anxious.

Faith is confidence in what we hope for and assurance about what we do not see.

—Hebrews 11:1

Do you have faith in God? Do you trust him? Trust is developed by cultivating your relationship with God. It requires knowledge and understanding of God's capabilities and his reliability. The kind of faith God wants you to have in him doesn't happen overnight. It is developed over time as you discover his magnificent attributes and watch him orchestrate the events of your life. How about that for a first-rate journey!

Your trust in God will grow as you walk with him every day and discover the depth of his incredible love for you. Then, as you continue to know him better, your beliefs will be grounded in what you have learned to be true.

Believe God knows what's best for you.

God created you. He fashioned every fiber of your being. He understands you better than you could ever hope to understand yourself. He knows every detail of your past and has a clear view of your future.

God can see the consequences of the decisions we make today, even years into the future. We, on the other hand, are anchored in the present moment. As a result, our choices are based on limited insight and are influenced by what we believe will bring immediate happiness. We assume that what makes us happy today will certainly be good for us tomorrow. Unfortunately, that is not always the case.

> The LORD says, "I will guide you along the best pathway for your life. I will advise you and watch over you."
> —Psalm 32:8, NLT

God sees the big picture of your life. He understands what is best for you much more clearly than you ever will. He knows who will be your perfect soul mate. Trust him to guide you with your decisions for what's best for you. The best is revealed through patience and perseverance, but it is always worth the wait.

Believe God is totally committed to your well-being.

God is love. He is faithful and kind. His grace is evident in all that he has done for us. God, in the person of Jesus Christ, was willing to endure unimaginable torment as he died on a cross for our sins because of his love for us. If he was willing to do that for us at a time when we were his enemies, how can we possibly question his commitment to us now that we are his children?

> If, while we were God's enemies, we were reconciled to him through the death of his Son, how much more, having been reconciled, shall we be saved through his life!
> —Romans 5:10

> "I know the plans I have for you," declares the LORD, "plans to prosper you and not to harm you, plans to give you hope and a future."
> —Jeremiah 29:11

Remember, God's best gifts aren't always wrapped in the pretty packages. God is more committed to your spiritual growth, development and maturity than he is to your immediate happiness. Sometimes the road is hard.

God is unconditionally committed to guiding your steps down a path custom-designed for your eternal fulfillment. That may be difficult to accept if that path currently has you walking through a deep valley of troublesome times. But trust him. Eventually you will find yourself on a peaceful mountaintop looking back and realizing that the current things in your life would never have been possible apart from the journey through the valley below. God is working through your circumstances to make you ready to meet your soul mate.

Believe God is absolutely trustworthy
to keep his word.

God is truth. What he says is reality, regardless of how things appear or what our feelings proclaim. It is Satan who raises doubts and distorts God's words. It is only as we focus on God's impeccable character that we gain the hope and confidence we need to believe the promises he has given us.

Let us hold unswervingly to the hope we profess,
for he who promised is faithful.
—Hebrews 10:23

God's promises will definitely be fulfilled. However, he is not bound by our timetable. God will do what he says when the time is right. Until that time, he expects us to wait with hopeful anticipation of the blessing to come. Trust that God is working in you and through you to accomplish his purposes in your relationships.

Believe God is able to change your situation
in an instant.

All too often, we are guilty of imagining our future based on what we see in our present situation. And yet we have all experienced fateful moments when, through some unexpected event, our life was forever altered.

God is the Engineer of our circumstances. He guides us through the routines of life until the time is right to interject the unexpected. Right now he is at work in the lives of other people on your behalf. He is orchestrating their circumstances, influencing their attitudes and guiding their actions. Then, at precisely the right moment, your lives will intersect and he will reveal his handiwork. And when he does, if you choose to look with your spiritual eyes, you will be gasping with amazement as you see what he has once again done on your behalf. Believe that God is working through your current situations to bring you to your soul mate.

Now to Him who is able to do exceeding-
ly abundantly above all that we ask or think,
according to the power that works in us.

—Ephesians 3:20, NKJV

Trust God more and rely on self-effort less. He is able.
He is willing. He is trustworthy. Spend time with him every day
so your trust in him will grow. While you are waiting for God to
introduce you to the love of your life, make sure you develop a
loving relationship with the Matchmaker. Then, by faith, you
will experience the best that he has in store for you—your ideal
soul mate!

APPENDICES

A

Soul Mate Compatibility Guide

A re you compatible? That is a crucial question! But as important as discerning your compatibility with a potential mate is, can you be completely objective in your evaluation?

Mutual attraction, infatuation and physical involvement will all influence your objectivity. Therefore, it's wise to carefully listen to the opinions that trusted family members and godly friends may have about a prospective mate. They are looking at the relationship from a distance and are sometimes better able to see what fits and what doesn't.

ARE YOU . . .

Compatible?
[Much the same]

Complementary?
[Balancing each other]

Clashing?
[Polar opposites]

How alike are you when considering the various qualities listed below? Are you compatible, complementary or polar opposites?

In which areas are you similar? Essentially, because of shared values, the decisions you would each make independently in these areas will not be significantly different.

Which differences are complementary? Do you balance each other? Are you actually better together than you are apart?

Are the two of you polar opposites in any areas? While it is true that opposites attract, it is also true that, over time, extreme differences can produce extreme frustration.

EXTERNAL QUALITIES

Consider the following external qualities. These are the more obvious traits that you notice about each other. These external factors can make you seem like a well-matched or odd PAIR to others.

External Qualities make you a nice PAIR:

Personality

Appearance

Interests

Reputation

Personality
- Openness   (imaginative, adventurous vs. conventional, traditional)
- Conscientiousness   (spontaneous, messy vs. structured, orderly)
- Extraversion   (social, verbal vs. reserved, quiet)
- Agreeableness   (sensitive, cooperative vs. skeptical, insensitive)
- Emotional Stability   (moody, reactive vs. calm, positive)

Appearance
- Age
- Ethnicity
- Body type
- Height
- Hair
- Hygiene
- Clothes

174

Interests
- Leisure activities
- Political activities
- Religious activities
- Health / fitness activities

Reputation
- Heritage / family background
- Successes / failures
- Popularity / fame
- Friends / acquaintances
- Status

INTERNAL QUALITIES

Now consider the following internal qualities. These inner traits are much less obvious initially and are discovered over time through communication and observation. These inner qualities are foundational to the development of long-lasting **SPECIAL** relationships.

Internal Qualities make your relationship SPECIAL:
    Spiritual maturity
    Purpose
    Expectations
    Character
    Intelligence
    Attachments
    Life experiences

The following is a partial list of issues affecting **SPECIAL** characteristics.

Spiritual Maturity
- Devotion to God
- Worship of God
- Consistency in walk with God
- Bible knowledge

- Theological beliefs
- Service
- Fruitfulness

Purpose for Life
- Ministry outreach
- Career advancement
- Community service
- Raising and helping progeny
- Building relationships
- Pursuit of pleasure

Expectations
- Behavior
- Children
- Companionship
- Finances
- Living conditions
- Retirement
- Romance / sex
- Work / careers

Character
- Attitudes
- Speech
- Actions

Intelligence
- Communication ability
- Level of education
- Desire for knowledge
- Demonstrated wisdom
- Creative ability
- Problem solving

Attachments
- Commitments to family
- Commitments to friends
- Commitments to church / ministry / mission
- Commitments to employer / job / career
- Commitment to pets
- Commitment to a geographic location
- Commitments to desires / goals
- Commitments to a cause

Life experiences
- Nationality / culture
- Parental relationships
- Major crises
- Major accomplishments
- Childhood experiences
- Teenage experiences
- Adult experiences
- Successes
- Failures

Move forward in a relationship with wisdom. What your initial feelings and emotions tell you is a dream match today, could change over time. Be realistic in your estimation. And because your objectivity could be compromised, trust the feedback and advice you receive from wise friends and relatives.

> Do not be yoked together with unbelievers. For what do righteousness and wickedness have in common? Or what fellowship can light have with darkness?
> —2 Corinthians 6:14

> Can two walk together, unless they are agreed?
> —Amos 3:3, NKJV

B

DOES IT SEEM HOPELESS?

Are you struggling with feelings of hopelessness? Have you started to wonder if you'll ever meet that special someone? Or maybe you've started wondering if such a person is even out there at all?

Don't be discouraged! God knows the desires of your heart and wants the very best for you. He is the only One who knows what is truly best. God's timing is different from our own, and "waiting on the Lord" is a strong theme throughout the Bible. Those waiting times can be some of our deepest, most meaningful times of fellowship with God. Jesus tells us to "seek first his kingdom and his righteousness" (Matthew 6:33) and to not be anxious.

Take advantage of this waiting time to get to know and trust God. A.W. Tozer, in his book *The Pursuit of God,* says, "God is so vastly wonderful, so utterly and completely delightful that He can, without anything other than Himself, meet and overflow the deepest demands of our total nature, mysterious and deep as that nature is." Have you experienced that yet? If not, we urge you to get to know him better!

Be encouraged by the verses listed below and trust that God hasn't forgotten you! He's right here with you—listening to you, loving you, desiring a closer relationship with you. Lean on his Word and his understanding in times of seeming hopelessness, and he will provide you with the love, strength and encouragement you need.

Why, my soul, are you downcast? Why so disturbed within me? Put your hope in God, for I will yet praise Him, my Savior.

—Psalm 42:5

Hope in the LORD; for with the LORD there is unfailing love. His redemption overflows.

—Psalm 130:7, NLT

Endurance develops strength of character, and character strengthens our confident hope of salvation. And this hope will not lead to disappointment. For we know how dearly God loves us, because he has given us the Holy Spirit to fill our hearts with his love.

—Romans 5:4–5, NLT

Be strong and let your heart take courage, all you who hope in the LORD.

—Psalm 31:24, NASB

You are my refuge and my shield; I have put my hope in your word.

—Psalm 119:114

Sustain me, my God, according to your promise, and I will live; do not let my hopes be dashed.

—Psalm 119:116

The eyes of the LORD are on those who fear him, on those whose hope is in his unfailing love.

—Psalm 33:18

Let your unfailing love surround us, LORD, for our hope is in you alone.

—Psalm 33:22, NLT

Put your hope in the LORD both now and for evermore.

—Psalm 131:3

Such things were written in the Scriptures long ago to teach us. And the Scriptures give us hope and encouragement as we wait patiently for God's promises to be fulfilled.

—Romans 15:4, NLT

LORD, where do I put my hope? My only hope is in You.

—Psalm 39:7, NLT

O LORD, you alone are my hope. I've trusted you, O LORD, from childhood.

—Psalm 71:5, NLT

I wait for the LORD, my whole being waits, and in his word I put my hope.

—Psalm 130:5

Rejoice in our confident hope. Be patient in trouble, and keep on praying.

—Romans 12:12, NLT

C

FEELING CONFUSED?

Are you feeling confused about your situation? Maybe you're just not sure how to relate in this sometimes crazy and chaotic dating world. Maybe you're just wondering why you haven't found anyone yet or why nothing seems to be happening for you. Is God still moving in this area of your life?

Wait! Stop everything! While it is easy to fall into this trap of doubt, remember it is just that: a trap. God is not the God of chaos or confusion. He brings clarity and confirmation to all our situations if we trust in and rely on him.

So, what do you do? First, don't trust your own feelings of confusion in this area. Lean on God and his Word for clarity and trust that he's right all the time.

Just as confusion is fed by doubt, so clarity is fed by conviction and belief. Use the verses below to help redirect your thought-life and focus on the clarity that God wants us all to have. We don't get to know the future, but we are blessed with promise after promise from his Word about our life. What happens next is up to him, but trust that he hears you, he sees you and he knows your heart.

> I will instruct you and teach you in the way you should go; I will counsel you with my loving eye on you.
>
> —Psalm 32:8

I will lead the blind by ways they have not known, along unfamiliar paths I will guide them; I will turn the darkness into light before them and make the rough places smooth. These are the things I will do; I will not forsake them.

—Isaiah 42:16

In all your ways acknowledge Him, and He will make your paths straight.

—Proverbs 3:6, NASB

This God is our God for ever and ever; he will be our guide even to the end.

—Psalm 48:14

Whether you turn to the right or to the left, your ears will hear a voice behind you, saying, "This is the way; walk in it."

—Isaiah 30:21

In their hearts humans plan their course, but the LORD establishes their steps.

—Proverbs 16:9

I am always with you; you hold me by my right hand. You guide me with your counsel, and afterwards you will take me into glory.

—Psalm 73:23–24

Your hand will guide me, your right hand will hold me fast.

—Psalm 139:10

The LORD makes firm the steps of the one who delights in him.

—Psalm 37:23

His God instructs him and teaches him the right way.

—Isaiah 28:26

D

GRIPPED BY FEAR?

Is the fear of loss or potential pain keeping you from a successful relationship? What about the fear of failure? Or the
fear of repeating prior mistakes?

If that's you, you're not alone. Most of us experience
those fears in the beginning of a new relationship. Sometimes
they are so consuming that we won't even allow ourselves to begin a new relationship. Hey, if there's no relationship, we can't
mess it up, right?

It's easy to forget that fear is just a tool of Satan to make
us miss our mark. On the other hand, if we keep our focus on
God and follow his leading, he will direct us. But we have to
know him to hear his leading! And honestly, it's not about us
anyway. It's about the will of God and what he has for us that's
important.

Use the verses below to help you get to know him better.
And trust that God's got everything under control. His love never ceases!

> Fear not, for I am with you; be not dismayed, for
> I am your God. I will strengthen you, yes, I will
> help you, I will uphold you with My righteous
> right hand.
>
> —Isaiah 41:10, NKJV

Have no fear of sudden disaster or of the ruin that overtakes the wicked, for the LORD will be your confidence and will keep your foot from being snared.

—Proverbs 3:25–26

The LORD is my light and my salvation—so why should I be afraid? The LORD is my fortress, protecting me from danger, so why should I tremble? When evil people come to devour me, when my enemies and foes attack me, they will stumble and fall. Though a mighty army surrounds me, my heart will not be afraid.

—Psalm 27:1–3, NLT

God is our refuge and strength, always ready to help in times of trouble. So we will not fear when earthquakes come and the mountains crumble into the sea. Let the oceans roar and foam. Let the mountains tremble as the waters surge!

—Psalm 46:1-3, NLT

I am the LORD your God who takes hold of your right hand and says to you, Do not fear; I will help you.

—Isaiah 41:13

God has not given us a spirit of fear, but of power and of love and of a sound mind.

—2 Timothy 1:7, NKJV

You have not received a spirit of slavery leading to fear again, but you have received a spirit of adoption as sons by which we cry out, "Abba! Father!"

—Romans 8:15, NASB

I sought the LORD, and He answered me, and delivered me from all my fears.

—Psalm 34:4, NASB

There is no fear in love; but perfect love casts out fear, because fear involves torment. But he who fears has not been made perfect in love.

—1 John 4:18, NKJV

He who listens to me shall live securely and will be at ease from the dread of evil.

—Proverbs 1:33, NASB

The LORD is my helper, so I will have no fear. What can mere people do to me?

—Hebrews 13:6, NLT

E

GOD DESIGNED YOU

Do you feel like a loser in the gene-pool lottery? Do you compare yourself to others and find yourself lacking? Do you wish you were someone else?

Knowing God designed you helps you understand the significance you have in his eyes. You are special. You are created in his image.

You are not an accident!

The Bible tells us that he formed each of us individually in our mother's wombs and that we are the work of his hands. What an amazing thought—how deeply we are known by the Creator of the universe!

Consider these verses and spend some time quietly pondering your significance in God's eyes.

> You created my inmost being; you knit me together in my mother's womb. I praise you because I am fearfully and wonderfully made; your works are wonderful, I know that full well. My frame was not hidden from you when I was made in the secret place. When I was woven together in the depths of the earth, your eyes saw my unformed body. All the days ordained for me were written in your book before one of them came to be.
> —Psalm 139:13–16

Know that the LORD is God. It is he who made us, and we are his, we are his people, the sheep of his pasture.

—Psalm 100:3

You guided my conception and formed me in the womb. You clothed me with skin and flesh, and you knit my bones and sinews together. You gave me life and showed me your unfailing love. My life was preserved by your care.

—Job 10:10–12, NLT

The Spirit of God has made me; the breath of the Almighty gives me life.

—Job 33:4

God created mankind in his own image, in the image of God he created them; male and female he created them.

—Genesis 1:27

From birth I have relied on you; you brought me forth from my mother's womb. I will ever praise you.

—Psalm 71:6

Before I formed you in the womb I knew you.

—Jeremiah 1:5

You brought me out of the womb; you made me trust in you even at my mother's breast.

—Psalm 22:9

Did not he who made me in the womb make them? Did not the same one form us both within our mothers?

—Job 31:15

From birth I was cast on you; from my mother's womb you have been my God.

—Psalm 22:10

F
GOD LOVES YOU

You want to be loved by someone special. You want someone to care about you and be committed to you. You want someone to be willing to make sacrifices for your well-being.

No person will ever love you more, be as committed to you or make a greater sacrifice for you than your heavenly Father. He loves you unconditionally and will do so forever.

When you understand God's incredible love for you, it rightly takes your focus off trying to fill your need for love through human relationships. It helps you to rest in his love regardless of your circumstances. Human love from imperfect beings will often fail you, but God's love is solid truth that will never fail.

Consider God's profession of love for you and let it become your constant source of assurance that you are loved.

> Nothing can ever separate us from God's love. Neither death nor life, neither angels nor demons, neither our fears for today nor our worries about tomorrow—not even the powers of hell can separate us from God's love. No power in the sky above or in the earth below—indeed, nothing in all creation will ever be able to separate us from the love of God that is revealed in Christ Jesus our Lord.
>
> —Romans 8:38–39, NLT

I pray that you, being rooted and established in love, may have power, together with all the Lord's people, to grasp how wide and long and high and deep is the love of Christ, and to know this love that surpasses knowledge—that you may be filled to the measure of all the fullness of God.

—Ephesians 3:17–19

I have loved you, my people, with an everlasting love.

—Jeremiah 31:3, NLT

Each day the LORD pours His unfailing love upon me.

—Psalm 42:8, NLT

"Because they love Me, My Father will love them. And I will love them and reveal Myself to each of them."

—John 14:21, NLT

"The Father Himself loves you, because you have loved Me."

—John 16:27, NKJV

With his love, he will calm all your fears.

—Zephaniah 3:17, NLT

He will love you and bless you.

—Deuteronomy 7:13, NKJV

G

GOD OFFERS YOU THE BEST

Our heavenly Father is committed to your well-being. Think about that ... God cares about you! Not only did he design you, but he also has mapped out a perfect course for your life that will result in your utmost joy and fulfillment. But it requires your trust in his goodness and your obedience of his directives.

Do you believe God has a wonderful plan for your life? Do you understand that the valleys of life always lead to mountaintops, if you are willing to follow God by faith?

Meditate on the following promises of God. Ask the Holy Spirit to embed these truths into your heart so they become unshakable convictions that will guide you to a glorious destiny.

> Many, LORD my God, are the wonders you have done, the things you planned for us. None can compare with you; were I to speak and tell of your deeds, they would be too many to declare.
> —Psalm 40:5

> "I know the plans I have for you," declares the LORD, "plans to prosper you and not to harm you, plans to give you hope and a future."
> —Jeremiah 29:11

> The LORD says, "I will guide you along the best

pathway for your life. I will advise you and watch over you."

—Psalm 32:8, NLT

The LORD God is our sun and our shield. He gives us grace and glory. The LORD will withhold no good thing from those who do what is right.

—Psalm 84:11, NLT

Even strong young lions sometimes go hungry, but those who trust in the LORD will never lack any good thing.

—Psalm 34:10, NLT

Trust in the LORD and do good. Then you will live safely in the land and prosper. Take delight in the LORD, and he will give you your heart's desires. Commit everything you do to the LORD. Trust him, and he will help you.

—Psalm 37:3–5, NLT

He fulfills the desires of those who fear him; he hears their cry and saves them.

—Psalm 145:19

May he give you the desire of your heart and make all your plans succeed.

—Psalm 20:4

"If you remain in me and my words remain in you, ask whatever you wish, and it will be given you."

—John 15:7

This is the confidence we have in approaching God: that if we ask anything according to his will, he hears us. And if we know that he hears us—whatever we ask—we know that we have what we asked of him.

—1 John 5:14,15

You have granted him his heart's desire and have not withheld the request of his lips.

—Psalm 21:2

H

ONLINE RESOURCES

Relationship with God

As a follower of Christ, you should be making your relationship with God your highest priority. A growing love relationship with God is critical to everything else that happens in the Christian life. Do you want to get to know God better and develop a closer relationship with him? Go to www.mypraize.com/group/soulmates/page/god.

The Holy Spirit

God has designed us for supernatural living, which is dependent on him for wisdom, power and resources available only through the Holy Spirit. Living our lives in the power of the Holy Spirit is an exciting adventure. God is waiting to flow his power through us so that we might accomplish his purposes. Find out more about how to be filled with the Holy Spirit and how to walk in the Spirit. Go to www.mypraize.com/group/soulmates/page/filled.

Overcoming Attitude and Behavior Problems

If you are repeating a particular sin again and again—and if you would be glad to give it up if you only knew how—then *Soul Prescription* is for you. Learn more about the five steps to true healing and freedom in *Soul Prescription* by Bill Bright and Henry Brandt. Begin the process of turning away from debilitating habits and embrace Holy Spirit–empowered virtues. Go to www.mypraize.com/group/soulmates/page/behavior.

Discerning God's Will

Are you trying to figure out what God's will and plan are for you? God has given us the freedom to make our own choices, but how do we make the right choices that will make it possible for us to experience God's best? Discover biblical principles and practical insights for discerning God's will. Go to www.mypraize.com/group/soulmates/page/decisions.

For more information about finding God's best for you, visit www.SoulMatesByGod.com.

Made in the USA
Lexington, KY
26 August 2018